Language and Communication

Language and Communication

Essential Concepts for
User Interface and
Documentation Design

AGNES KUKULSKA-HULME

New York   Oxford

Oxford University Press

1999

Oxford University Press

Oxford   New York

Athens   Auckland   Bangkok   Bogotá   Buenos Aires   Calcutta
Cape Town   Chennai   Dar es Salaam   Delhi   Florence   Hong Kong   Istanbul
Karachi   Kuala Lumpur   Madrid   Melbourne   Mexico City   Mumbai
Nairobi   Paris   São Paulo   Singapore   Taipei   Tokyo   Toronto   Warsaw

and associated companies in
Berlin   Ibadan

Copyright © 1999 by Agnes Kukulska-Hulme

Published by Oxford University Press, Inc.
198 Madison Avenue, New York, New York 10016

Oxford is a registered trademark of Oxford University Press

Library of Congress Cataloging-in-Publication Data
Kukulska-Hulme, Agnes, 1959–
Language and communication : essential concepts for user
interface and documentation design / Agnes Kukulska-Hulme.
p.   cm.
Includes bibliographical references and index.
ISBN 0-19-510838-8
1. User interfaces (Computer systems)   2. Electronic data
processing documentation.   I. Title.
QA76.9.U83K85   1999
005.4'37—dc21   97-41640

9 8 7 6 5 4 3 2 1

Printed in the United States of America
on acid-free paper

Preface

This book has been written with the intention of opening up the field of language and communication to people who are involved in computer application and documentation design, who are concerned about making their systems understandable to users. It shows how important concepts from this field can be applied in practice to improve design, so that users do not have to experience the frustration and bewilderment that is all too common when interacting with existing applications, "help" facilities, and manuals. No previous knowledge of language-related terminology is assumed on the part of the reader.

The task of describing a range of language and communication concepts to students, specialists, and professionals working in other fields—broadly speaking, in user interface and documentation design—has been a compelling enterprise. I have a very strong empathy with computer users and a fervent belief that language is a key element in human-computer communication. This conviction comes from experience training humanities students in the use of information, interaction, and communication technologies and from designing and evaluating computer applications for other nontechnical users. The original impetus for this book came from my doctoral thesis on users' language in relation to the task of information retrieval from documentation on computer security (Kukulska-Hulme, 1993). This book covers a far broader area and gives readers the means to address a wide range of problems.

English is not my first language, and I have taught and studied other languages along the way. I have come to view all computer users as being, in a sense, language learners: A new application environment creates new meanings for terms which, as users, we perhaps thought we already knew, but that now turn out to have a different meaning. It also introduces new terms and concepts. I wanted to describe what happens in that situation. By looking, in turn, at each of the essential concepts used by linguists—meaning, context, function, variety, equivalence, and so on—and at concrete examples of these concepts in the language of the computer user interface, I have drawn what I hope is a detailed picture of how language shapes users' understanding of what is happening within an application and what they think they are able to do. It also determines their capacity to make full use of its facilities and functions.

This is a new perspective, different from that offered by academic and professional colleagues who specialize in the psychology of language use in human-computer interaction.

The following readers will find the book especially relevant and helpful:

- *computer professionals*, especially application designers and developers, and operating-system user interface designers
- *usability specialists* and human factors specialists
- *technical authors*, information developers, writers of training materials
- *writers* of independent user guides to popular applications
- *educational software designers*, educational technologists, instructional system designers
- *students* following courses in computer science, cognitive science, communication science, human-computer interaction, and artificial intelligence
- *students* of technical writing and professional and business communication
- *academic, industrial, and commercial researchers* in the computer and cognitive science communities
- *technical managers* involved in system prototyping and development or in documentation development
- *Web site designers*, both amateur and professional

Acknowledgments

The idea for this book was conceived while I was working as Lecturer in Computational Linguistics and French in the Department of Languages and European Studies at Aston University in Birmingham. It was developed and greatly enhanced in my new province as a lecturer in the field of educational technology at the United Kingdom Open University in Milton Keynes.

My thanks go to colleagues who commented on parts of the book at various stages, especially Open University editors Sue Glover and Jane Moore, who gave me valuable detailed feedback on part of an early draft, and Robin Mason, Head of the Centre for Information Technology in Education. Reviews drafted by Robert Rodman and anonymous reviewers for Oxford University Press were both encouraging and very helpful in refining the content. Stephen Woods helped to start the important work of building the indexes. A special thank you goes to my husband, Tony—a daily "How's the book?", along with unceremonious critical comment, made all the difference.

Registered Trademarks

Terminology

- the term "user interface design" is frequently used as shorthand for "user interface and documentation design"
- in chapter 10, the term "designer" is used to refer to anyone who has to design and develop a user interface or to write user documentation

Contents

I

INTRODUCTION AND FOUNDATION

ONE

Introduction

Language in Interface and Documentation Design

Language and Computer Users

When asked about the purpose of human language, most people would instinctively reply that its main purpose is communication. Most of us take for granted our ability to communicate easily through language. It would be natural for us, as computer users, to expect the same degree of ease when we interact with systems and user manuals. But even computer professionals and other experienced users are often baffled by the explanations that appear in so-called "help" facilities; perplexed by the meanings of words in menu options, on toolbars, and buttons; and hampered in information retrieval by having to use terms that do not readily express their needs.

Words on the computer screen can create a barrier to communication, yet users who turn to help files or documentation are frequently disappointed. *Times* columnist Lynne Truss speaks for many when, at the end of yet another unrewarding session on her computer, she declared: "I have even stopped looking at those files titled 'Read This,' because it's sad but true: I have never yet opened one whose contents I could understand" (1996).

Often, a frustrated cry of "I don't understand the options on the screen" leads many users to just "try it and see what happens," with potentially disastrous or time-wasting consequences. "I don't understand the manuals" is another typical refrain, which provides an excellent reason for not reading them. It has been said so often (e.g., Smith 1992), that alternative ways of informing or teaching users are now being promoted; for instance, video training. This mode of delivery can make information more palatable, but it does not eliminate the problems created by confusing use of language in the user interface.

3

The difficulties experienced by both professional and casual or new users are not inevitable; they are not something to be accepted as a feature of computer systems, manuals, and on-line documentation. Something *can* be done to improve the way that language is presented and used in these contexts. This book provides the necessary communicative framework as well as practical recommendations to make it possible to significantly improve user interface and documentation design.

The fundamental problem is that effective communication is not automatically assured every time we speak or write, so we cannot assume that just because a computer application displays and allows use of language, or that a manual is written in a language the developer and user both know, the messages they carry can be understood. Furthermore, an overtly friendly style of writing, which has transformed some recent user manuals and guides, can mask the fact that when it comes to the crunch—actually putting the information into practice—users find they have not fully understood the instructions and are none the wiser.

Communication through language is about presenting a comprehensible message to the user, as well as understanding people's use of language. It must be distinguished from the related activity of natural language processing (NLP) as a fundamental concept. Computer specialists involved in NLP systems—for example, automatic or computer-assisted translation, automatic abstracting, and text generation—may have no experience designing for language-based communication, since these types of system are not predominantly interactive. Language specialists collaborating on various computer projects often have a largely traditional background in linguistics, with a bias toward systematic descriptions rather than effective communication, and toward work based on textual or speech data containing a considerable amount of "'considered' language, written to simulate speech in artificial settings" (Sinclair 1991, p. 16). The traditional approach is largely rule- and sentence-based, which makes language and its meanings seem easy to control, so it is not surprising that it should be so readily adopted by some computer specialists. Up until now, the communicative language side of systems has been overlooked, both in research and practice. For users, this often means having to struggle with systems that seem hostile or exasperating.

The most constructive stance we can take in designing the user interface is to regard all computer users as *language learners*, since every new application environment creates new meanings for familiar terms and introduces new terms and concepts. Considering what appears on the screen and in user documentation as a "new language" for the user can make one question beliefs and assumptions about what users will or will not understand. It also introduces a productive aspect to language: Users certainly need to understand, but they also need to be able to produce language appropriate to the application in order to get the most out of its use.

Making a Difference: Examples of Bad Practice

For readers who do not yet see clearly the relevance of language and communication awareness to interface and documentation design, several examples of common problems follow. Other difficulties are discussed in greater detail later in the book. It is sometimes necessary to put oneself in the shoes of an inexperienced user to best appreciate these problems.

Examples given here are drawn from the following sources:

- popular word processing, spreadsheet, and presentation software: WordPerfect 5.1, Word for Windows 6.0, Word for the Macintosh 4.0, Lotus 1–2–3 Release 5, Excel version 5, and Powerpoint version 4
- CD-ROMs for interactive learning: Microsoft's Encarta Multimedia Encyclopedia (1994 and 1997 World English Edition) and Cinemania'94 Interactive Movie Guide
- desktop help facilities: Mac OS balloon help
- IBM proprietary applications on networked systems

In the inevitable instances where new software versions with an altered user interface supersede the versions referred to in the examples, the essential points being made will remain valid for other applications, other designers, and other information developers.

Throughout this book, examples are drawn frequently from the user interfaces of word processing and document handling systems. These systems constitute an area of common experience that most readers will readily relate to as computer users. This helps to avoid lengthy descriptions of systems so that simple, general points about the language can be made. Further research will be needed to investigate the applicability of particular observations across a wide range of application types, which is beyond the scope of this book. Here we are concerned with breaking new ground: understanding the nature of the problems observed and establishing the language concepts that will help designers develop solutions to those problems.

Four types of problem are explained and illustrated:

- problems with meanings and explanations
- language that disregards reality
- structures that hinder comprehension
- problems of language in retrieval

Problems with Meanings and Explanations

The interface to WordPerfect, one of the most widely used word processing (WP) packages, is full of words that have special meanings within the application that differ from their meanings in general, everyday language. For this reason, the terms *styles, characters, blocked* lines, and *global* searches frequently baffle WP users. Users already have an idea of what these words might mean, and when they come to use the software, they have to change their previous conceptions. In a similar vein, Lotus 1-2-3 uses the expression "to expand the highlight"; in this case, *expand* and *highlight* may be known from other contexts. The challenge for the user is to try to understand the new (specialized) meanings of familiar words encountered previously in everyday life or in other computer applications. In help facilities, where there is potential for adequate explanation, these terms may be listed out of context, with their definitions leaving the user none the wiser. For example,

style = a combination of formatting codes and/or text

In addition, *circularity* of definitions (when the definition contains the word being defined) is sometimes a problem. For example, in Lotus 1-2-3 help:

EDIT = 1-2-3 is in the *edit* mode

in Word for Windows "status bar" text (which gives a description of icons):

AutoFormat: Automatically formats a document

To improve this situation, the language of explanation and definition should be understood and properly applied. The relevance of context, meaning change, and users' prior knowledge of language should be considered. These concepts are elaborated on in parts II and III of this book.

Concepts of *synonymy* and *equivalence* come into play when words of similar meaning are used close to one another. For instance, the Macintosh desktop can be used to display so-called "aliases"; when "balloon help" is activated, pointing to the word *alias* produces the following text (emphasis added):

This is an *alias* to an application. To open the application, open this alias. To drag an item to the application, drag it to this alias. Change the *icon*'s name by clicking on the name and typing.

In this context, *alias* and *icon* are close in meaning, and unless one is totally comfortable with the meanings of these words, it is confusing to see both of them used with reference to what appears to be the same item.

Similarly, Program Manager Help in Windows 3.1 (Box 1) has a section about organizing applications and documents where seven of the words in the brief screen text refer to what appear to be very similar things:

applications	icons	program items
documents	properties	windows
files		

Organizing *Applications* and *Documents*

Using Program Manager, you can organize your *applications* and *files* into groups that make sense to you. For help with organizing *applications*, choose one of the following topics:

- arranging *Windows* and *Icons*
- changing *Properties*
- copying a *Program Item*
- creating and deleting groups
- creating and deleting program items
- moving a program item

Box 1. Text on a Program Manager help screen in Windows 3.1 (emphasis added)

It is also curious how *applications* and *documents* become *applications* and *files*, which then become just *applications*; so how does one organize *documents*?

Language That Disregards Reality

Problems arise when a user is faced with language that does not take into consideration everyday patterns of expression or real-life situations. In popular applications, it is not unusual to find difficult words used rather than their more ordinary equivalents. One example of an inflated formulation is "To perform an action on a file"; other examples are given in Box 2.

If this is a preference for abbreviation (in these cases, using one word rather than two), then the consequences must be understood, since the "longer"

WordPerfect:

- to *view*, rather than *look at*
- to *import*, rather than *bring in*
- to *remove*, rather than *take away*
- to *restore*, rather than *bring back*

Lotus 1-2-3:

- to *invoke*, rather than *call up*

Box 2. Difficult words and more ordinary equivalents

verbs, of Anglo-Saxon rather than Latin origin, are much more common in today's English and may be preferred by users. If the single words seem more like "real terminology," then it is time to examine the concepts of terminology and special languages. We have to ask ourselves: Are verbs like *create* and *generate* (*create a document, generate a table*) everyday words or computing terms? Are they indispensable in a word processing system? How does *make* compare?

In a similar vein, an IBM proprietary computerized calendar application (or *diary* in British English), in which the user can select actions from a menu, includes these choices:

- deleting an item from the calendar
- inserting an item into the calendar
- moving an item
- copying an item

We all have calendars or diaries, but we do not talk about them in these terms, not even in formal business situations. We are used to making appointments, changing appointments, canceling them, crossing them out, scheduling meetings, making sure a meeting does not clash with any other meeting, seeing if someone is available, and so on. Similarly, instead of "adding multiple items to a calendar," we plan regular appointments and holidays; instead of "viewing calendar items," we look at details of appointments. The language is integral to the application; an appreciation of terminology and language psychology will help developers choose more appropriate interface language.

The Help section of Encarta Encyclopedia contains instructions for finding a topic using its "Contents" facility. The instructions say:

> To find the topic you want:
> 1. (. . .)
> 2. Begin typing the topic name in the box above the list.
>   *The list moves to words beginning with the letters you type*

A complete list of help topics can also be accessed. One of these topic headings is:

> The Main Window: what does it do?

Outside the world of computers, *lists* do not *move* and *windows* do nothing at all; they only have things done to them. These different conventions are assumed, and the language reflects this. Here it is useful to understand the relationship between language and background knowledge or reality, which includes the use of *metaphors* (names transferred to objects to which they are not properly applicable), in order to realize that assumptions are being made. It is also helpful to be aware of the *grammar* of words, especially the fact that certain words go together: in this instance, what normally happens to a list (one makes a list, one chooses from a list, etc.) or what usually happens to normal windows (one opens and shuts them, looks out of them or through them, puts plants in them, etc.). We might then decide to say: "As you type, the list moves up or down in the window to allow you to choose words beginning with the letters you type"; or "What can you do in the Main Window?" In a later version, Encarta 97, the list "scrolls as you type," which is more succinct but assumes familiarity with scrolling on the screen. This problem raises the question of whether understanding an object (e.g., a *list*) entails knowing how that object behaves and how to talk about the object (e.g., you make or read a list, a list can move, a list can scroll while you are typing somewhere else on the screen) in any language.

Structures That Hinder Comprehension

Another widespread tendency is to overload words by piling on modifiers. Modifiers are words that change the meaning of other words. Adjectives often do this; e.g., *executable* modifies *file* in the term *executable file*. When the modifiers are strings of nouns or combinations of adjectives and nouns, this results in complex structures that can be difficult to decode for those who do not use them on a daily basis. If you are not familiar with the language of insurance, you may be puzzled by a phrase like "the *optional comprehensive policy improved no claim discount* protection" (modifiers in italics). Less extreme examples of this type can be found in the language of computing. For instance, the Powerpoint Help facility talks about "the *Word-wrap Text In Object* check box"; additional examples can be found in Lotus 1-2-3 and Excel spreadsheet Help facilities, as shown in Box 3.

Excel:

- the *Reenter Protection Password* box rather than *the box* for reentering a protection password

Lotus 1-2-3:

- the *pointer-movement* keys rather than *the keys* for pointer movement
- a *label-prefix* character rather than *a character* for prefixing labels
- the *upper left corner* cell rather than *the cell* in the upper left corner

---

Box 3. Complex structures with modifiers

This problem is especially familiar to users whose first or native language does not allow such structures (e.g., French), so that an extra decoding or "unpacking" effort is required. Thus, it would be useful to reflect on the position of modifiers, given that overloaded terms can pose comprehension difficulties. The need for each modifier should also be examined; for example, does a *protection password* give greater or different security than a *password*, or is protection the function of every password? An appreciation of psychological and cognitive aspects of language comprehension is relevant at this point, and the role of *redundancy* in language must be considered.

Unfamiliar sentence structures, influenced by the information processing model in which lists, conditions, and statements based on logic are commonplace, present another type of problem to the user. The descriptive contents section of the Cinemania Interactive Movie Guide states:

> *To see a list of movies only*, biographies only,
> or topics only, use the buttons just below the list

In line with more typical, everyday English, this could be rephrased as: "*If you want to see just a list of movies*, just biographies, or just topics. . . ." Unfamiliar structures often make it necessary for users to read a sentence more than once to understand its meaning.

Problems of Language in Retrieval

A different example may show how a communicative approach would make a difference in information retrieval. This comes under the heading of "user-centered" indexing (Fidel 1994) in contrast to indexing and retrieval that are document-centered. We can refer to a case study in this area (Kukulska-Hulme 1993, 1996a). When information is being retrieved from a collection of documents, words and phrases are used to summon relevant texts or passages. Assume that a user is unfamiliar with the documents and perhaps also with the subject area. The words and phrases he or she will want to use to extract information will not be exactly the same as those that occur in the documents or their associated indexes. This is a common problem. In this case study, users of the IBM AS/400 system formulated queries relating to the security of their system. When the language of these queries was examined, it was found that the words and phrases that had been used did not match those in the index to the computer security manual or those of the relevant on-line information system. Box 4 shows that even when one knows the relevant index entries, it is not possible to know which index entry is likely to lead to an answer to a specific query. It became clear that users had information and knowledge needs that could be observed in their use of language, but because their use of language was not being taken into consideration, their needs were not being met. The indexes were full of precise words relating to specific technical solutions, while the users were expressing themselves in much more imprecise, problem-oriented language.

Recognizing the communicative purpose of index items would have made a difference to the design of those indexes. Retrieval is about answering questions and understanding something about the nature of questions: how to recognize the underlying intention and translate it into suitable search terminology. For example, in the following question:

How can I prevent someone from looking at my letters?

How can I and *prevent* are important to the user because they concern method and intended action; instead, the index offers *document password* as an entry point to the answer to that question. A user might also ask:

Can I restrict access to sensitive files?

where *can I* (possibility), *restrict* (action), and *sensitive* (category) all reveal the user's underlying intentions. When it is necessary to find ways of linking questions to answers, the following points are helpful:

- being aware of the communicative purpose of *parts of speech* (verbs, adjectives, etc.)

User queries:

- How can I prevent someone from looking at my document?
- How can I stop someone accessing my office documents?
- Can I restrict access to sensitive files?
- Can users' confidential mail be accessed by any other user?
- Can I look at other peoples' electronic mail?
- How do I give access to only certain documents in a folder?
- How can I be sure no one can access my documents that are confidential?
- I want to stop people viewing spool yet be able to control printers.

Relevant index entries:

- document password
- document user profile
- files, logical and physical
- spool control special authority
- spool job user profile
- spool user profile

Box 4. Mapping difficulties around the notion of confidentiality

- being able to categorize *concepts*, e.g., "people" concepts; the notion of confidentiality
- knowing something about the relationships of *specialized terms* to everyday words, e.g., "authority" versus "right"

In this section, we have reviewed a few examples of the problems created by computer interfaces that are not well designed from a language point of view. In parts II and III, examples of both good and bad practice are shown and relevant concepts are explained in detail.

A Communicative Approach

The communicative approach proposed in this book is based on concepts from the field of linguistics, the science of language. This field may be unfamiliar to many readers, and it may come as a surprise that language study can be classed as a science. Crystal explains:

> Linguistics shares with other sciences a concern to be objective, systematic, consistent, and explicit in its account of language. Like other sciences, it aims to collect data, test hypotheses, devise models, and construct theories. Its subject matter, however, is unique: at one extreme, it overlaps with such "hard" sciences as physics and anatomy; at the other, it involves such traditional "arts" subjects as philosophy and literary criticism. The field of linguistics includes both science and the humanities, and offers a breadth of coverage that, for many aspiring students of the subject, is the primary source of its appeal. (p. 412)

People readily understand what it takes to learn a foreign language, but not many have had the opportunity to consider language itself—as a system, as a field of enquiry, or, in its broader setting, as a means of communication. The communicative approach is a particular way of looking at language; it emphasizes the act of using language. It is concerned with identifying communication purposes and strategies and the language elements used to put them into practice. It deals with the rhetorical, social, cognitive, and psychological aspects of language understanding and use. Like any other discipline, linguistics has many branches and trends that cannot be detailed here; issues related to communication are of special interest within psycho- and sociolinguistics and other interdisciplinary human sciences, for example, anthropology.

To understand users' problems with computer systems and documentation, we have to know about different aspects of language: the way it works; the way it looks and sounds; the way it changes and renews itself; its shades of meaning; varieties; and its social and individual effects. We have to consider the need for communication (e.g., instruction, explanation), communication contexts within and outside of language, and the constraints of speech or writing. This knowledge can help to explain why communication has failed in a given situation, and it can help to anticipate and avoid the problems in the design of future systems.

As Evans et al. put it in *User Needs in Information Technology Standards* (1993), "computer literacy . . . is a diversion. Instead we need *people literacy*—that is, computers designed to be human-literate so that the people who use them can simply get on with their job" (p. 227; emphasis added). Currently, users are largely expected to adapt their means of expression to what is required by the computer system, but this will certainly change. To make systems and documentation better at communicating with the user, computer specialists can strive to become "people literate" (as suggested by Evans), and "language literate," in the sense of being more aware of essential language concepts and the effects of language in use.

New interface technologies have not eliminated the need to use language in the majority of applications. In parallel with the process of proliferation and penetration of computers into all aspects of life, improved interface technologies have helped to bring users with no technical or computing background into everyday contact with computers. On the whole, this evolution has not included a proper consideration of the role of language in on-screen and user manual interactions. There is some evidence of change: "As a part of user-centered design, the terminology in user interfaces should be based on the users' language and not on system-oriented terms" (Nielsen 1993, p. 123). Many otherwise excellent books on human-computer interaction (HCI) deal with human language only in passing or to a small extent. Yet from a user's point of view, language on the screen is an essential ingredient of an interface—arguably *the* essential ingredient, since it is present on practically every screen in every application.

Is it not very telling that the index to a major 600-page volume on *Usability in Practice—How Companies Develop User-Friendly Products* (Wiklund 1994), to which some 17 companies have contributed chapters, contains no entry for "language," none for "communication," and just one for "linguistics," which is mentioned briefly as an "aspect of psychology"? Language does get reasonably extensive treatment in Helander (1990), but this is a most substantial tome—over one thousand pages in its paperback edition, as big as a telephone directory—which surely cannot be digested by any busy practitioner or student.

At present, the development of *natural language interfaces* is a specialized area of computer science rather than an aspect of all systems that comprise language-based interaction. Dutta lists some conditions under which natural language interfaces are not desirable; for example, when "the content and type of interactions are limited (so that menu type interfaces can perform the functions easily and efficiently)" (1993, p. 184). But current menu-type interfaces are often complicated and inefficient from the user's point of view.

A menu interface is a summary of functions available to the user; similarly, a search index and a list of topics (contents) are brief representations of what is available. In a system that has all three facilities, it is possible for a user to experience them as a tyrannical triangle: hopping from menu to index to topic list and back again, unable to get the required information. Plowing through manuals or screenfuls of help text is equally unsatisfactory. Instead, users should be helped to build up their knowledge, so that an access point such as an index entry becomes a starting point for the construction of a portion of knowledge.

The Convergence of Technical Writing and Interface Design

With the trend toward electronic publishing and the greater self-reliance of computer users who are turning to on-line help, databases of queries or frequently asked questions, and tutorial facilities (where previously a "technical expert" might have been called in to help), it is worth noting the convergence of the two activities of technical writing and human-computer interface design. The technical author—who may be known as an information developer or designer—was able in the past to postpone the planning of retrieval mechanisms, such as the index of a manual, to the conclusion of a writing project, but now has to think much earlier in the process about how the information will be consulted, since it may be made available on-line, and so there is a need to think about designing the retrieval aid in parallel with the documentation. In turn, the application or interface designer now has to consider usability and the provision of helpful information on—or "behind"— the screen, in a way that mirrors some of the tasks of the technical writer. Editorial and typographical design skills are also very important in today's user interface design.

Systems that allow users to experiment with new ways of working, such as collaborative writing, electronic conferencing, or accessing of information over global networks, call for a design effort that encompasses the skills that technical writers, editors, and HCI specialists have to offer. The multilingual, multicultural dimension of these systems makes it all the more important that those involved should have some training in the language communication aspects of interface design and an appreciation of what it might be like for a nonnative speaker of English to use an application requiring an understanding of the language. Many new applications will have to be designed with an international body of users in mind.

"HCI is undoubtedly a multi-disciplinary subject," say Dix et al. (1993, p. 3), pointing out that the ideal designer of an interactive system would have expertise in a whole range of subjects, including psychology, cognitive science, ergonomics, sociology, computer science and engineering, business, graphic design, technical writing, and others. Language science is not mentioned as a separate discipline, though one imagines it is assumed to be a part of psychology, sociology, and technical writing. The present book should demonstrate that language is the one missing link between interface and user in current thinking and practice.

Language at the Interface: Design Constraints

The conditions under which application systems and documentation are designed and developed impose a number of constraints that cannot be overlooked. In particular, "support" for the user in terms of explanations of one kind or another can seem like a dispensable extra, especially if—and this is likely to be the case—end users have not specified it as part of their requirements. Language support provided at every stage of use of an application is not as tangible as a separate help file or manual in commercial terms, so it is less likely to be provided. But from a management point of view, especially in large-scale projects, application systems that communicate effectively with users in terms of unambiguous options, explanations, or guidance can be cheaper to implement than systems that require users to attend training programs followed by intensive on-going human support. Nielsen (1993) has stated that "usability is a comparatively cheap way to improve product quality" (p. 9).

The features and style of an existing operating system are undoubtedly the most significant constraint on language in the interface to new applications. As a rule, applications must use an operating system's functions and must be consistent with its language and its style. Operating systems are the place where good interface design should begin. If real change is to be allowed to take place, it is up to the computer industry giants who develop the most widely used operating systems to reconsider their approach to language in interface design.

Other constraints must also be acknowledged; for example, in off-the-shelf software, the diversity of users makes it difficult to implement any user model. Availability of space on the delivery medium, whether screen or print, can also present a problem that may call for a degree of ingenuity if it is to be overcome. Other constraints have to do with human language itself: Technical language, which must be used in many cases, is quite inflexible compared with everyday language. It has a specific set of terms in any given subject, and it is called on to perform a closed set of functions (e.g., instructing the user), and these in turn are associated with conventional means of expression. Conventions in expression and in conceptual or visual design can, of course, turn out to be self-imposed constraints. For example, we can ask ourselves whether access and support mechanisms such as an index and a glossary have to be arranged and situated as they currently tend to be (arranged alphabetically, separated from the main body of information) or whether there are other ways of dealing with these important resources for the user. On the other hand, when there is no convention, many interpretations are possible:

What does it mean for an application to have a "help" facility, for instance? "Help" can mean several things, including information, advice, step-by-step instructions, prompting, troubleshooting, and tutoring.

Bearing in mind current design practice, there is often a need for generic terms at the higher levels of selection in the interface to an application: *file* may serve this purpose in relation to *text, document, graphic, database, table,* and so on. In this type of situation, it may not be possible to find a totally satisfactory generic term from a communicative point of view. *File* has become a ubiquitous interface term, but it is possible to be more careful about how its meaning is presented to users. A less hierarchical design may be called for in some cases or one that does not hide more meaningful, lower level terms and phrases from the user. This comment is also applicable to indexes and other retrieval mechanisms intended for users, which should prioritize the communicative value of language rather than its convenience value. The aesthetic aspect—what is pleasing to the eye—is also often at odds with the communicative approach. It need not always be so: Typographical expertise can be called on to make text look attractive. In any case, priorities of values in the user interface have to be worked out for any new development project.

In distributed systems, where the interaction is predominantly between a number of users working collaboratively in computer-supported collaborative work (CSCW) or contributing their views to a forum, there is less emphasis on language-based interaction with the computer application that mediates communication. Yet this is deceptive, for in that type of environment, language problems are not dispelled and may even be intensified. Davis (1995) has written that opportunities for ambiguity "increase in mediated domains and reach their peak in the new telemedia environment" (p. 517). Ambiguity can arise from new social roles created by the environment and is reflected in messages produced within it. The role of the user interface is to address this problem of ambiguity and to provide various means of supporting human interaction where it is desired (i.e., where ambiguity is not deliberate).

As the face of computing continues to change, there is an ongoing need to review the influence of language on the user in relation to other means of communication. For example, some multimedia systems appear to efface the textual medium, while graphical displays, icons, and direct manipulation systems seem to do away with the need for language. In reality, is language ever completely absent from such systems? It is doubtful. If we examine these systems more closely from the user's point of view, there is nearly always the need to elaborate and explain visual images. In some applications that have a graphical user interface, if a user "hovers" over an icon, an explanation of its function comes into view—although language is not immediately visible, it has not been eliminated. Language also improves accessibility for people with visual disabilities, with the use of screen reading software: text labels associated with graphical images (Vincent 1997).

In the future, it is possible that a user will not have to control the computer explicitly, but rather the computer will observe the user and act accordingly. It is also very likely that users will not need to think in terms of running applications. Despite these developments, there will continue to be a requirement to provide a level of subtlety and complexity in communication that is only afforded by human language. The balance of communication modes and media will continue to change, but language is certain to remain a significant element in the majority of human-computer interactions.

Aims, Relevance, and Contents of This Book

Aims and Relevance

The fundamental aim of this book is to introduce a communicative view of language for the improvement of human-computer interface and documentation design. This view is both a fresh perspective on design and, most importantly, a starting point for developing an agenda that designers will need to be able to think about and discuss language and communication issues in professional circles within the computer industry and with users. The book also aims to develop two major arguments: first, that all computer users should be seen as language learners, and second, that nonnative speakers of English who are users of English-language software have special language needs that need to be accommodated in any user interface.

The concepts that are presented here, that give a different focus to each chapter, have been selected from the considerably wider field of "language and communication," as represented in books such as Fromkin and Rodman (1993). They have also been reinterpreted in the context of user interface and documentation design. The wider field deals with topics such as the origin of language, the mechanisms of sound production, child language development, writing systems, and many others. The concepts presented here also differ from ones that might be found in a traditional book on linguistics: Books up through the 1970s cover traditional themes such as word, sentence, and meaning structures, whereas newer books include discussions of the "pragmatic" level of language—language use and communication—but in a theoretical rather than an applied framework. Mey (1993) is full of practical examples of language in use but is not specifically related to computing. As a word of caution, some books in the field of language and meaning are not for the majority of practitioners; for example, Andersen (1990) is a work of advanced theory, inaccessible to the average system designer, who would not gain much from having communication defined as "a presupposition from an act or set of acts, whether symbolic or non-symbolic, to a symbolic act or object, based on a semiotic schema" (p. 119)!

As well as presenting concepts by describing, explaining, and questioning, this book aims to present practical examples of problems in interfaces and documentation following them up with recommendations and resources. Linguistic terminology is used, but the emphasis is firmly on concepts, principles, and applications. Special attention is given to concepts used in HCI literature that have particular meaning from a language and communication point of view, for instance, "context," "jargon," and "metaphor." At the same time, there is an attempt to broaden the designer's repertoire of useful concepts, especially including "language variety," "equivalence," "language change," and "verbal context"—concepts that are prominent in current language learning literature and textbooks, but which do not yet enjoy common currency in HCI research and practice. Some examples of language problems are from software reference books and user guides published independently of software companies and manufacturers, particularly those written with the nontechnical user in mind. The book aims to educate and to stimulate reflection, and the reader should soon become persuaded that even small changes, based on a better appreciation of language, can result in an improvement in design. For readers who are interested in this field, attention is drawn to areas where further research is needed to support or extend our knowledge of the language problems experienced by users.

Language is more important in some types or aspects of computer systems than in others. The need for the highest standards in safety-critical systems is perhaps the most evident. Generally speaking, the problems are most acute in facilities intended for users who are not computer specialists. Two categories where language really matters are general-purpose, "off-the-shelf" software, and learning or tutoring aspects of systems.

In the first category, *off-the-shelf software*, the challenge is to make the language suit all users, irrespective of their background, experience, and the field of application. Word processing, spreadsheets, and database packages are typical examples. Here, the software interface is in a sense separate from the user application, and use of the software requires acquaintance with the language of the interface.

The second category, *learning and tutoring facilities*, includes all systems where a user is learning an application and is particularly sensitive to being hampered by difficulties in communication. This category comprises interactive tutoring systems, Help facilities, "troubleshooting" or problem analysis, on-line assistance for information retrieval, query languages, and multimedia systems. Some of the education and entertainment software destined for the home market falls into this category.

The language interface problem is also highlighted in systems used by people worldwide for whom English is not their first language. Successful translation of the interface into other languages, where required, depends on the quality of the original text. One of the key problems of translation is ambiguity. Another important aspect is an appreciation of the cultural and social underpinnings of language.

Understanding the user is fundamental to system and documentation design, and this book should help those computer professionals who have to grasp the specialized languages spoken by such computer users as accountants, bankers, pharmacists, lawyers, scientists, and many others.

Overview of Contents

As we come to the end of this introductory chapter, it may be helpful to outline the contents of the rest of this book.

Chapter 2 (part I) introduces the foundation concepts underlying all discussion of language in a communicative context, so it sets the scene for what is to follow. Key points are summarized at the end of each section.

Chapters 3–7 (part II) relate to language in general and cover concepts such as variety, change, and the notion of equivalence. The role of context, the effect of written, spoken, and visual media, and the intricacies of interaction are all dealt with. These issues are discussed with reference to the problems of interface and documentation design, with practical examples, design recommendations, or lists of relevant words from existing user interfaces.

Chapters 8–9 (part III) present specialized languages; for instance, languages for particular purposes and functions, such as labeling, abbreviation, explanation, and assistance. Again, practical examples, resources in the form of word lists, or recommendations are given for each concept as appropriate.

Chapter 10 (part IV) contains guidance in how to go about putting the ideas in this book into practice. It is a summary of the key points made throughout the book about the implications of a communicative language orientation for user interface and documentation design and gives more recommendations.

Further readings and language resources are suggested in the Appendix.

Two indexes, a subject index and an index of words commonly encountered in the interface to operating systems and applications (e.g., *file, form, copy, open*) close the book. The second index will allow designers and technical writers to check what has been discussed here about particular words that are to be incorporated in new user interfaces or user documentation.

The book deals mainly with written (visible) language, but elements of spoken language are discussed, especially to contrast the two and to show how one influences the other.

The text has been written in such a way that a "spiral" effect can be observed: concepts are introduced briefly, later to be examined in ever greater detail, with reference to other concepts. A number of themes or threads are developed throughout, and this is made explicit through cross-references in the text as well as in the subject index. This allows for both sequential and selective reading, while recognizing that chapters are not entirely self-contained. Some concepts are very closely related: For example, it is not desirable to discuss *context* without reference to *meaning* and vice versa. The idea is that it should be possible to build up one's knowledge of concepts and the relationships between them. The book can also be used as a reference volume, and the two indexes provide additional quick entry points.

So now we are ready to start laying the foundations of an understanding of language and communication. Chapter 2 introduces some fundamental concepts in a spirit of questioning and reflection.

TWO

Foundation Concepts

- Why is communication a risky undertaking?
- When do computer users find themselves at a loss for words?
- Why does it matter that words go together in pairs?
- Are there words that are never spoken?
- Can someone know a great deal about a word without understanding it?

This chapter begins to shed some light on fundamental issues connected to language. It explores the above questions and introduces some conceptual distinctions that will help in understanding the more specific, applied notions considered in parts II and III.

The core concepts are *communication*, *function*, and *meaning*, and these are explained along with other important related terms.

Grammar is discussed in a communicative perspective, and language is set in the context of other modes of communication and in relation to reality (a philosophical issue, tackled here strictly from an applied language angle).

Communication: Language in Action

Most of us know that the language we speak, English, for example, is not really one language but many—due to regional variations, for instance. Most people are also aware of qualitative differences: "good" and "bad" English. This value judgment is the basis of what can be described as *a prescriptive attitude to language*. "Correct" spelling, punctuation, and grammar immediately spring to mind. The prescriptive view has it that there are certain standards and conventions to be maintained, in order to protect or preserve the language or for the sake of good communication. Accuracy, consistency, and avoidance of jargon are often quoted as qualities of English that enhance communication. Advice on how to achieve these qualities can be found in "guides to style and usage," such as Gowers (1954). Cameron (1996) is a recent academic work that discusses the issue of "correct" language in a balanced way.

Although advocating "correct" usage, some of the style guides stress the fact that they are against pedantry or language dictatorship. This more liberal approach to language correctness is a relatively recent development. Simon Jenkins notes that: "Guidance that might once have been mandatory is often now permissive" (1992, p. 6). Gone are the days when we would be admonished for believing that grammar could be "relaxed at will" and consequently branded as "unduly conceited or mentally lazy" (Metcalfe 1975, p. 12)! On the other hand, it is generally accepted that in technical or specialized usage, precision and consistency are still essential features. Many computing terms have strict definitions, stipulated in dictionaries and in national and international standards issued by relevant bodies (e.g., British Standards Institution, American National Standards Institute, International Standards Organisation).

The rate at which the field of computing is growing reveals the difficulty in keeping up with the task of defining terms. Also, until fairly recently, it was unusual to see definitions that departed from a prescriptive, authoritative stance. This is the case in Williams and Cummings' explanatory dictionary for the nonspecialist reader, in which their definition of *hardware* begins with the words: "Hardware refers to those parts of the computer that you can bump into, such as the printers, drives, modems, etc. . . ." (1993).

A book published ten years earlier entitled *Computer Confidence—A Woman's Guide* adopted a similarly informal approach in a chapter that covers basic computer vocabulary. Box 5 shows one definition from the book and another taken from the *Macmillan Dictionary of Information Technology.* They are written in two contrasting styles, and their content and structure are also rather different.

"The success of Information Technology will depend, ultimately, upon the readiness of society to communicate and cooperate . . ." say the authors of the same *Macmillan Dictionary of Information Technology* in the introduction to their work, "It is our hope that this dictionary will assist by lowering a few of the barriers to communication." What were these barriers in 1985, and are they still the same today? The authors allude to the convergence of different fields and technologies and how that makes communication between people from various specialist backgrounds difficult. They also point out that at the time of writing, information technology (IT) was only just emerging as a discipline in its own right. "At the outset of the compilation (in 1980) the authors were conscious of the continuing role of the traditional technologies in this field, and the fact that the jargon of the old technologies tends to fuse,

Network: A computer network lets people connect remote terminals to computers or computers to computers. The computers and terminals can actually be wired together or they can use a standard phone line by attaching a modem and telephone to the computer. The computers send signals over the phone line. (Heller and Bower 1983, p. 118)

Network:

1. a series of interconnected points
2. in communications, a system of interconnected communication facilities
3. in data structures, a structure in which any node may be connected to any other node (Longley and Shain 1985, p. 232)

Box 5. Two different styles of definition for different readers

and confuse, in the new." The disciplines that they decided to include were printing and publishing, computers and databases, networks and communications, photography and cinematography, television and recording, microelectronics and software, word processing, and business systems. In a later edition (3rd ed., 1989) the authors comment that the language of IT is constantly evolving, and that by 1989, printing terms, for instance, had assumed a more important role than previously, due to the popularity of desktop publishing. As many of these fields combine today in multimedia and multifunctional networked environments, new sets of terminologies emerge, delimited according to new criteria (e.g., professional tasks and functions) rather than fields of origin.

Generally speaking, in computing or IT, language is used in a controlled way, which implies conciseness, explicitness, and the use of accurate, unequivocal terminology. Artificial languages and codes are the epitome of language control and are essential in system-centered communication (e.g., between machines, sometimes between system designers, or in some types of human-computer dialog). Language control is not the total answer to all the problems of communication, but it does have a part to play.

Although we may not always agree with the prescriptive approach to language, we can at least readily see its purpose. For many people, the same cannot be said of linguists' attempts to *describe* language, unless perhaps it is done with a view to teaching language. However, there is another important motive for description: *discovery.* Computers can aid discovery by allowing us to process large volumes of language samples (texts, recordings) in order to reveal exactly how people use their language—as opposed to how we think they use it. This means, for example, that we are able to find out more about computer users by processing and then describing their language. We can discover what words and phrases they habitually use, how they describe their problems and concerns. This can inform language communication choices in interface design. (See the appendix for details of projects that enable the analysis of collections of texts and spoken language samples.)

Language description takes in all aspects of a language, including the psychological and social perspectives. Traditionally, description was associated with structure: The purpose of describing a language was to reveal its underlying structures (e.g., how words or sentences were put together). Presently, it is much more usual to see language in its cultural, social, and personal contexts, so that to describe a language is also to describe the people who use it and the situations in which it is used. The language of a computer interface must be seen in its *personal context* (the user), its *social context* (e.g., the professional or home environment in which the system is used), and in its broader *cultural* and *intercultural contexts*.

Prescription and description both have a part to play in improving *communication*. Prescription sets norms for communication, while description throws light on actual use. Interactive systems have produced a need for a reappraisal of the factors in effective communication. Communication is, above all, language in action; it emphasizes the people or information systems engaged in the interaction, the language that is their medium, and the success (or otherwise) of the event.

In computing terms, communication is about transmitting a message, a conception based on a mathematical theory of communication, which emphasizes the physical aspects of the act: sender, receiver, noise, and so on. We know that in human terms, communication also has to do with intentions, expectations, presumptions, and inferences. According to Milroy (1986), writing on this subject in a book whose overall theme is "the art of listening," a miscommunication may be said to take place "when there is a mismatch between the speaker's intention and the hearer's interpretation" (p. 18). It is well known that an important mechanism in language for ensuring good communication is *redundancy*. Milroy (1986) reaffirms this: "Constant repetition and repair are important components of communication in context" (p. 18).

Saugstad (1977) makes another significant point: The activity of communicating something and the activity of understanding what is being communicated are different. In particular, understanding is dependent on precision: "the individual cannot understand what is meant by something which is not specified in some definite way" (p. 219). Milroy (1986) tells us more about understanding by explaining that that there are two kinds of miscommunication—*misunderstandings* and *communicative breakdown*:

> misunderstandings are not perceived as interrupting communicative efficiency, and it is probable that many more misunderstandings take place than are ever discovered. Communicative breakdown on the other hand occurs when one or more participants perceive that something has gone wrong. (p. 25)

As observed by Brown et al. (1994), communication is a risky undertaking, "requiring not simply the exchange of linguistically packaged ideas, but *an effort of imagination* on the part of the reader or listener . . . (p. 5; emphasis added). Human-computer communication must take account of the human aspects, which are always bound up with the situational context and the purpose of communication. Sager (1994) has written at length about the elements of a communication theory for specialized communication in the context of language engineering and translation; he has this to say about communication purpose:

> Communication . . . is a conscious and deliberate and hence purposeful human activity. For scientific and technical communication the purpose can be simplified by stating that it is concerned with affecting the knowledge structure of the participants. (p. 51)

Scientific and technical communication (STC) differs from communication in other spheres in that it places a particularly high value on dispassionate, impersonal, factual writing and speaking. Traditional STC texts, such as articles, reports, catalogs or almanacs give information but typically do not engage the reader in an interaction or a cooperation (a two-way process). It is true that the traditional nature of STC texts is changing, with the use of the World Wide Web to publish and discuss research articles, to interact with and update cataloged information, and so on. We also need to note that, in a wider sense, the user interfaces of computer applications create a special environment for technical communication, one that combines the formal aspects of STC with the human and social aspects of interaction. This is an area that will require further research before new models of communication can be described in a satisfactory way.

Those who compile bilingual dictionaries are keenly aware of one further dimension of communication: cultural references:

> To understand and communicate successfully, one must be culturally as well as linguistically competent. . . . Language and culture are inextricably linked. (Back, 1996, p. 2)

We will come back to this point when we consider the idea of linguistic and cultural equivalence in language and the effect of context—including cultural context—on language and communication. "Culture" has, of course, a particular meaning in relation to the user interface, where the usual literary and historical references do not play a part, yet where both designers and users are aware of the existence of a special culture.

In brief:

- prescriptive norms and descriptions of language both have a place in the process of designing the language of the user interface;

- a communicative perspective gives particular emphasis to language users and the problems they may encounter;
- human-computer communication must take account of intentions, expectations, presumptions, and inferences;
- redundancy is an important mechanism for ensuring good communication;
- computer applications create a special environment for technical communication, one that combines formal aspects with human, social, and cultural aspects.

Focus on Function

From a communicative point of view, it is important to notice the functional aspects of language: its purpose in any given situation. Knowing about the structure of a language is not in itself sufficient to explain how people learn it and use it. *Structural* information concentrates on the components of a language (e.g., sounds, words, sentences, meanings), on its rules (e.g., how new words are formed, what word order is possible), and on the formal relationship between meaning and its expression. *Functional* aspects emphasize the act of acquiring a language, or a subset of it, and putting it to use. However, it must be said that structure and function are not unrelated, for each determines the other. This relationship is further explored in the next section.

In general terms, it may be said that language serves to represent ideas, and at the same time it has an expressive dimension that reflects its personal and social nature. Its two essential functions are the *representational* and the *expressive*. For example, the word "friend" represents a person (usually!), but it also expresses a human relationship; this is not to say that both functions are necessarily discernible in every sample of language.

On a more detailed level, different types of language-based communication may be identified, depending on what we are trying to achieve. Language presents us with infinite possible ways of using it. These can be referred to as "functions of language" and can be related to specific situational purposes of communication. For example, if our aim is to give clear instructions, to persuade someone, or to offer help, we choose our words and sentences to help us achieve that purpose. In short, we are taking advantage of a possible function of language to fulfill the purpose at hand. The actual linguistic choices we make in the process of realizing our purpose are "language in use" (see Box 6).

Function, purpose, and *use*—words that are used interchangeably in everyday conversation—are therefore not exactly the same. We should add that the term "function" is used in many different ways in linguistics, including the

> - possible functions of language: instructing, assisting, persuading, etc.
> - purpose at hand: e.g., to assist the user
> - language in use: e.g., *Do you need some help?*; *Press F1 for Help*; *Help Topics*

Box 6. Function, purpose, and use of language

analysis of the functions of the different parts of a sentence, which may be called "functional roles" [e.g., as used by Halliday (1975)].

These distinctions become clear when we see that it is possible to have a purpose in mind but fail to achieve it because the language used is not right for that purpose—it is inappropriate. An example of this is failing to communicate the meaning of a computing term to a user because the definition is too convoluted or contains words unknown to the user. To talk about language "in use" (language usage) is to consider it within a concrete situational context, in which communicative intentions are put into practice and have— or fail to have—a desired effect on the participants of a particular act of communication. The formal linguistic term for this aspect of language study is *pragmatics* (Mey 1993; Leech 1983; Green 1989).

With reference to the act of communication, the functions and purposes of language are similar to the "intentions" of a speaker or writer. "Function" tends to be used with respect to language, subsets of language, or samples of language (e.g., texts); "purpose" is often related to a situation (e.g., a professional situation); "intention" signals a human dimension, involving motivation and conscious will.

In the design of a user interface to a computer system, or of printed documentation, it is necessary to foresee or imagine the communicative act that will take place between the system and the user, making a point of clarifying and specifying the purpose of language use in the foreseeable range of situations, from both the system's and the user's points of view. Naturally, there may be more than one purpose in any given instance.

In brief:

- adopting a communicative approach means finding out about the functional aspects of language, rather than just its structural aspects;
- it is helpful to note that function, purpose, and use of language are not exactly the same;
- appropriate language is language that is matched to the purpose of communication;
- imagination is required of all those who take part in the act of communication.

Changing Meanings, Changing Forms

In language as a whole and in identifiable units or "chunks" of language, a conceptual distinction may be made between *meaning* and *form*, a form being the representation of meaning in sound or graphic symbols, such as the words on this page. Meaning and form can be thought of separately, but from a theoretical perspective they represent two sides of the same coin or constitute one linguistic "sign" (this concept was introduced by the linguist Ferdinand de Saussure). Meaning should therefore be conceived as a property of form, not as a separate entity. As Sinclair (1991) put it, "form is often in alignment with meaning" (p. 7); each time we consider a different form, the meaning is likely to change as well. However, in specialized subject fields, meanings (or rather "concepts") are traditionally represented as entities in their own right and are specified by means of definitions or diagrams.

The essential relationship between meaning and form is thought to be *arbitrary, determined by convention,* and *subject to change*. It is something that has to be learned. According to Halliday (1975), a child "learns to mean long before he adopts the lexical mode for the realization of meanings" (p. 9). Adults, too, can find themselves in situations where they do not have the necessary lexical resources to express what they mean; for example, when they do not know the specialized terms of an unfamiliar discipline, such as computing or leading-edge developments in computing.

So, even though it is possible to consider form and meaning from a structural perspective (What forms are there? What meanings are there?), the evolutionary aspect of their relationship to each other makes the relationship dependent on language variation and change—in a social context (change in convention) or in the individual (process of learning). In other words, meaning and form are related, but that relationship is always changing.

For many of the meanings we want to express, there are a number of forms—words, combinations of words, sequences of text—that could be used. Similarly, a function may be expressed through different structures. Sometimes it is in the process of selecting words that we circumscribe or qualify our fuzzy meanings [see also Kukulska-Hulme and Knowles (1992)]:

> *In everyday life:*
> That's odd—in fact, it's astounding.

> *In computing:*
> I need to copy it—I mean, I need to move it.
> Do you have a copy—a backup?

Each of the words, whether written or spoken, will very likely have a range of meanings, applicable in a range of contexts:

an *object* could be an aim, a focus, an item, an entity

Context—in linguistic terms being surrounding words or a situation—in fact helps to narrow down meanings. Out of context, words can be *ambiguous*. Some of their meanings may have been around for a long time, while others are recent additions or subtle alterations. The range of possible meanings, as recorded in dictionaries, for instance (where many words are described as being *polysemous*—having more than one meaning), is reduced to one actualized meaning in each specific context:

> the *object* of the exercise,
> *objects* of the imagination,
> the *object* of her desire,
> a number of unusual *objects*,
> *object*-oriented programming

Linking back to the representational and expressive functions of language, we can assert that meanings are ideas with an expressive capability. Words conveying value judgments and emotions (e.g., *incompetent, corrupt, disaster, satisfied*) are the most visible examples of this capability.

In brief:

- a word's meaning can change depending on context and passage of time—the relationship between meaning and form is conventional, not fixed;
- nevertheless, meaning and form are always very closely related;
- ambiguity of meaning is most likely to arise when words are presented out of context;
- for the computer user, the meanings of words will change or become more refined in the process of knowledge-building—learning about the application.

Grammar as Patterns in Language

"Stop pedaling if you feel pain, dizzy, or faint" says a notice on an exercise machine in a gym. Does this sentence sound right? Is its meaning obvious? Is it correct? It depends on whether we mean grammatically correct, so it is worth taking a closer look at what is meant by "grammar" and how it relates to meaning and vocabulary. We shall try to show that it is not helpful to create antagonism between vocabulary and grammar, even though they are not the same. "Grammar means lexicogrammar; that is, it includes vocabulary" (Halliday 1978, p. 39).

We tend to associate meanings with words, the vocabulary of a language (*lexical* or *lexicosemantic meaning*), but meaning is also expressed through smaller and larger units, from one meaningful sound (e.g., "Oh?") through to a whole text. It is something that is constructed out of the building blocks available in the language. How that construction takes place is a process that is not totally understood or agreed upon by linguists. It is possible to think of it as a process governed by rules—grammatical rules—but this is not the only way. Since the beginning of the 1980s, a particular trend in linguistics, *discourse analysis*, has taken center stage, overturning traditional approaches to grammar. In the expression "discourse analysis," the word "discourse" can have the same meaning as "text," but sometimes it is used by linguists "to underline the interactive, communicative purpose of a text" (Hoey 1991, p. 270), or it can be used specifically in relation to speech. Most notably, discourse analysis is concerned with chunks or "stretches" of language (Cook 1989) larger than the sentence—whole conversations, whole texts. Under the heading of grammar, topics such as discourse structures and conversational strategies are tackled (see Monaghan 1987; Longacre 1983; Connor and Johns 1990). Today, many linguists and language teachers see grammar as "patterns in language," which are patterns of vocabulary or co-occurrences of words. Words often go together in pairs or longer sequences (e.g., to *follow instructions*, to *repair damage*, to *choose* an *option*, an *open program*, an *error message*, the *update process*), and these patterns emerge gradually, as the discourse unfolds. The words form patterns differently depending on variables such as language function, variety, and the spoken or written medium (compare the patterns for the word "click" in different language varieties in Box 7).

Words are dependent on other words to define their role. For example, the role of a verb is to indicate an action, a state, or an occurrence, but *click* is not necessarily a verb, as can be seen in the examples given in Box 7. Adjectives (e.g., *normal, last, previous*) and adverbs (e.g., *regularly, completely, last, again, then*) are especially dependent on other words, in that their role is to qualify verbs, nouns, as well as other adjectives and adverbs—they do not normally stand alone. A hierarchical pull-down menu structure can mistakenly imply roles for words:

File

New

Open

This suggests *a new file* and *an open file*, when the intended meanings are probably *make a new file* and *open an existing file*. Microsoft Works 3.0 for Windows avoids this problem in the File menu by having the options *Create New File* and *Open Existing File*. Other applications provide explanations for each menu option as the user points to it; for instance, Lotus Freelance Graphics 2.1 for Windows gives the expanded version (*Create a New File*, etc.) just

From the language of computing:
    double-*click* a document
    click the triangle next to the folder's icon
    clicking an icon selects it
    Shift-*clicking*
    faster than *clicking*
(as used in Lon Poole's, *Macworld System 7.5 Bible*, 1994)

From everyday language:
    it *clicks* shut
    it finally *clicked*
    the lock opened with a *click*
    the cameras were *clicking*
    we seemed to *click* as soon as we met
    he *clicked* his fingers

From technical language:
    click and ratchet

Box 7. "Click" in three language varieties

above the menu, using color to draw attention to it. Microsoft Word 6.0 for Windows gives additional text in a status bar at the bottom of the screen. Unfortunately, this status bar text is too far away from the menu—people have been known to use the software for weeks without noticing the fact that the status bar changes!

A similar situation can be found in the Start menu on a Windows 95 desktop, which has options involving *new* and *open*:

New Office Document
Open Office Document

The second one means *Open an existing Office Document* (not *Create an Open Office Document*). Experienced users will have no problem with this because it has become a strange but common convention in *File* menus in popular applications. However, the general principle here is that new users, or any potential users evaluating a new system with a view to purchase, need unambiguous terms (e.g., *Existing Office Document*) or failing that, the additional clarity provided by extra words. How these words are displayed is mostly a matter of appropriate visual design and also a question of the importance accorded to explanations.

A set of options that mixes different parts of speech (members of different grammatical classes) is generally unhelpful: Box 8 shows part of an IBM AS/400 menu in which option 7—*Release processing*—is unclear. Is *release*

```
┌─────────────────────────────────────────────┐
│                                               │
│          Administrative Processing            │
│                                               │
│     Select one of the following:              │
│                                               │
│        1. Remove documents from DASD          │
│        2. Release pended work packages        │
│        3. System services processing          │
│        4. Print processing                    │
│        5. Update profiles                     │
│        6. Move platter                        │
│        7. Release processing                  │
│                                               │
└─────────────────────────────────────────────┘
```

Box 8. Part of an IBM AS/400 menu:
"Release processing" (emphasis added)

a verb, like it is in option 2, or is it a noun, in the mold of "system services" in option 3?

Thus, context is often needed to define a word's role (and with it, its meaning), yet context does not always show which role a word is playing: sufficient context is needed. The example in Box 9 uses the word *last* to illustrate this point. It is an issue that will be mentioned again when we look at the effect of context and at the problems of writing with a view to translation into another language.

To come back to our original example ("Stop pedaling if you feel pain, dizzy, or faint"), *feel pain*, *feel dizzy*, and *feel faint* are valid patterns in language. Presumably they have been combined along the lines of "if you feel *tired*, *hungry*, or *thirsty*"—three adjectives in a row; in this construction, we know that each of the three adjectives must be associated with "feel" in order for the statement to make sense. But "pain" is a noun, "dizzy" is an adjective, and "faint" could be a verb (along the lines of "if you feel pain or collapse").

```
┌──────────────────────────────────────────────────────────────────┐
│                                                                    │
│   Compare:  the last option                                        │
│                                                                    │
│        the most recent option?      ("last" as an adverb)          │
│                      OR                                            │
│        the only remaining option?   ("last" as an adjective)       │
│                      OR                                            │
│        the final option in a list?  ("last" as an adjective)       │
│                                                                    │
│   with:  the option selected when you last used the Edit menu      │
│                                      ("last" as an adverb)         │
│                                                                    │
└──────────────────────────────────────────────────────────────────┘
```

Box 9. "Sufficient" context for the word *last*

In this specific example, as readers of the notice, we use our world knowledge to interpret the correct meanings, so there is no need to worry about the parts of speech in this construction. However, in other cases where special subject knowledge is needed, it may be impossible to make the correct interpretation. So, for the writer or interface designer, what is important in this type of special subject discourse is not so much knowing whether one's writing conforms to rules of grammar, but whether the patterns that help readers (computer users) to understand the writing have been made available to them —whether the patterns are visible or can be made visible if required. Invisible, incomplete, or mismatched sets of language patterns can be confusing, difficult, or even impossible to translate with confidence into another language.

Apart from the idea of patterns in language, which is well established in current language teaching and learning practice (and will be developed in a later section on verbal context in chapter 6), there are some grammatical concepts of a more traditional nature that all interface designers should understand. Cutts (1996) is a good brief reference source for some of the important ones. One traditional concept is that of the *passive voice* (e.g., "this test *is recommended*," as opposed to the active form, "I recommend this test"). Much has been written in various books on technical writing about the use of the passive voice, and many style guides discourage its use. The advice is often misunderstood or ignored, not least of all because it comes under such an off-putting label as "passive voice"! "We don't know who or why" would be a more descriptive phrase! *No entries were marked*, says a message at the end of a process that the user expected the system to carry out. What happened? Why were no entries marked? Who should have done the marking?

One of the hidden dangers in the use of the passive voice is that its negative form ("This test *is not recommended*") can be especially ambiguous. In this example, are we *warning* someone not to do the test, or are we simply *stating* that the test does not belong to a specified set of recommended tests, but is still OK to do? By comparison, "I don't recommend that you do this test" is not ambiguous at all. There is a difficulty in using active forms on the screen without giving the computer anthropomorphous qualities, but there is usually a satisfactory solution. For the first meaning (warning) we might say, "Don't do this test" or "Don't use this test." For the other meaning (stating a fact), it is a matter of reformulation, depending on the exact context: "This is not one of the recommended tests."

Another useful traditional grammar concept is that of *modality*. Modality relates to the use of language to specify attitude, and particularly notions of possibility, probability, certainty, ability, permission, necessity, and obligation. Words like "can," "could," "may," "should," and "must" fall into this area and are important both from the point of view of their psychological effect on computer users and for understanding the essential constituents of the questions that users formulate in their minds as they go about the business of using an application. Correct interpretation of sentences with modals can be difficult:

> *may not* = might not OR cannot
> *cannot* = could not OR can never

An example from Microsoft Word is *Word cannot switch applications.* The *Collins Cobuild Student's Grammar* (Willis 1991), a book intended for learners of English, has a good section on modals that details the categories involved and the language elements used to express them.

In brief:

- newer approaches to grammar are functional and focused on discourse;
- words occurring next to one another, or within a short distance of each other, emerge as patterns in discourse and provide typical contexts;
- typical contexts and sufficient contexts help to define a word's role and its meaning;
- an understanding of some more traditional grammatical concepts, such as the passive voice, and modality, is also useful in user interface design.

Relationship of Language to Sound, Gesture, and Vision

While it may be said that language plays a central role in human communication, it is part of a wider scheme of modes of communication and "systems of signs." The study of this broader field—linguistic signs and all other possible types of sign systems—is the field of *semiotics.* The language "system" interacts with other systems, and in humans the various senses play their part, such as hearing, speech, and vision.

Sound production is very much an integral part of language, since words usually originate in speech. This means that a large proportion of new words come from the spoken language and are later used in writing. Abstract or specialized terms may, however, originate in writing and may be voiced only rarely or not at all. For example, a word like "tailorability" may be used in writing [in a chapter on programming by Winnett et al. (1994)], while the spoken equivalent might be "the ability to tailor" a system. In Microsoft Word for the Macintosh, there is a *Format* menu with a *Change Case* option which, according to its "balloon help" explanation,

> changes the *capitalization* of selected text

The word "capitalization" is not normally used in speech—we talk about typing or printing "in capital letters" or "in capitals."

Words are founded in speech in that when we read or write, we tend to "speak" the words silently, without saying them aloud. A computer user trying to figure out what to do in an application will silently read any words that are on the screen, normally from the left of the screen to the right (e.g., in English), and these words should "sound" right, both individually and as a sequence. Words that sound right are easily pronounceable and meaningful. Box 10 illustrates the problem of unusual words that are awkward to pronounce (to *unnest* as the opposite of to "nest"; a button that *subscripts characters*—"subscript" is not normally a verb). Box 11 shows examples of compound words that result in meaningless sequences: *Create a new word processor* or *Create a new communications*.

The implication for interface design is that words that are to appear on the screen should be read out loud to ensure they sound correct. Sequences of words and phrases resulting from consecutive selections that may be made by the user or from possible combinations of options should also be read aloud at the design stage.

In speech, features such as variations in sound (e.g., a rise/fall in pitch or loudness or a change in speed/tempo) signal new information or an emotional state and can have an effect on meaning. These *prosodic* features are largely unavailable in writing, although some can be expressed through the use of punctuation (e.g., !??) or description (e.g., "he thundered"). *Paralinguistic* features include the character of one's voice (squeaky, husky, etc.). *Intonation* (the melody of a phrase or sentence) can also carry grammatical information (e.g., turning a statement into a question or a command). Without the help of features of sound, there can be ambiguity:

Open—a statement or a command?

Meaning may be further altered through nonverbal communication signals or gestures: raising one's eyebrows, shrugging the shoulders, pouting, looking blank, and so on. A speaker's physical position in relation to a listener will determine the perceived importance or formality of a message, such as standing up while talking to people who are seated, compared with sitting with them. Traditionally, written messages have tended to be more official than spoken ones. Established communication media, in contrast with newer technologies, have certain conventions that determine how we perceive the

> *Unnest* paragraph
> *Subscripts* characters below the baseline

Box 10. Microsoft Word for the Macintosh— "balloon help" for specific icons

```
Create a new

    Word Processor   Spreadsheet   Database   Communications
```

Box 11. Part of Microsoft Works 3.0 *Startup dialog* screen text

message and that also make it easier to assimilate: These will include the lay-out and typographical features of information on a page and the turn-taking practice of a spoken or written exchange (e.g., a letter). In more modern computer interfaces, graphics often seem to dominate, and it is worth noting that new users' familiarity with the special visual mode of communication is assumed.

In brief:

- language is one of a number of means of human communication and is linked to hearing, speech, and vision;
- sound as well as nonverbal communication signals have an effect on meaning;
- the lack of sound in written language contributes to the problem of ambiguity;
- words that are to appear on the screen, including sequences of words and phrases, should be read aloud to ensure they sound correct.

Relationship of Language to Reality

There are two basic ways of "knowing" a word: The first way is being aware that the word exists (but not necessarily knowing precisely what it means), and the second way is understanding the word. We may know some specialized terms in the first way, for example, *VHS, nuclear fusion, osmosis*. In computing, terms like *ftp, encapsulation, connectionist, semaphore* may be known in a superficial way, depending on one's level of knowledge. A novice word processor user may know terms like *format, font*, or *retrieve* in a superficial way.

On the other hand, understanding a word is knowing its *referent*—what it refers to, which may be a concrete object or an abstract notion. Some words do not have an identifiable referent, because they are used to express relations (e.g., "as," "over," "to"); in that case, the word refers to a relation. Understanding may also involve knowing a word's *connotations*—its implied meaning and its associations in the minds of speakers of the language. These are often culturally-bound references. Words like *resume (résumé), conference, review, dictionary, diary*, and *reception* all have elements of cultural connotation. *Index* is used in some cultures in the sense of a *table of contents*. An index to a Web site can consist of a list of headings that looks more like a traditional table of contents than a word list. Mention a *computer conference* or a *chat facility* to someone who is new to these terms, and they will generally assume that spoken language is involved, which need not be the case.

Sometimes we know a good deal about a word without knowing the referent or understanding its connotations. This occurs, for instance, when we have encountered the word in a number of contexts, so we know what other words and structures typically accompany it, but we have still not worked out its full meaning. When starting out in word processing, we may have heard people talking about *style sheets, predefined styles*, and *standard styles*, we may have seen menus with options to *create, modify, apply styles*, and so on, yet all this does not mean we have ever seen, experienced, or used a "style."

Similarly, we may be able to assign a word to a group or class of words (e.g., it resembles words X and Y, it seems to be the opposite of X, or it is a verb), still without knowing its exact meaning. An inexperienced computer user might find this with the following sets of terms:

> byte, kilobyte, megabyte, gigabyte
> teleconferencing, telematics, telepointer

We discover then that words have relations with other words of the language as well as within actual sentences, where they are known as *syntagmatic* relations.

As we observe the ways that words form patterns in discourse, we are able to build up pictures in our minds about the typical or possible behaviors of objects, events, their attributes, and so on. In everyday life, we have fairly complete mental pictures of this sort in relation to everyday objects and happenings. As computer users, we may have to build up these pictures when faced with a completely new application, except that when we come across familiar-looking words (e.g., "list," "index," "style"), we may assume, often wrongly, that we already have some of the necessary knowledge. The language interface should, whenever possible, assist in this process of *relevant* knowledge-building.

Language is a part of reality, and the construction of reality is also achieved through language. "Reality" is a very broad term that needs to be subdivided if it is to be a useful concept in any applied view of linguistics. Our basic reality is our "self," our personal experience, knowledge, capacities, and personality. There is then our immediate environment where we interact with other people and, for example, with computer systems. In a wider sense, these interactions take place in a cultural reality determined by geographical location and by professional constraints. Situational and cultural "context" is most people's preferred term for situational and cultural reality.

In brief:

- when a person "knows" a word, it may be in a way that is incomplete and insufficient, since there are different ways and aspects of knowing;
- knowledge about a word can be built up by reference to other words in the language as well as by taking account of situational and cultural context;
- when users come across familiar-looking words, they may assume that they know them; the language interface should assist in the process of building relevant new knowledge about each word.

Having established in this foundation chapter the meanings of some of the underlying concepts and terms, we move on to part II, where five aspects of language are addressed: variety, change, equivalence, context, and medium. These have been chosen as being particularly relevant to user interface and documentation design.

II

ESSENTIAL LANGUAGE CONCEPTS
AND THE USER INTERFACE

THREE

Language Varieties

- Is jargon meaningless?
- Is a "requirement" the same as a "need"?
- Why might we never know that we failed to put across a message?
- Are user manuals ever "too chatty"?
- Do all speakers of English think alike?

This chapter addresses these questions and others. It is the first in a series of chapters that present various language concepts and show the ways they are applicable to user interface and documentation design. This part of the book is oriented toward developing a deeper understanding of language and a better appreciation of the needs of users as language learners, as explained in chapter 1.

Here we explore the concept of *variety* in language and look at the reasons or motivations behind variety. Distinctions are drawn between *colloquial* and *formal* and between *general* and *professional* language. Special consideration is given to *scientific* and *technical* language and to *jargon* and *slang*. The requirements of *international communication* are discussed with reference to English, and finally, we look at how variety is related to *writing style*.

Motivations in Variety: Habit and Purpose

"Creatures of habit" is a label that seems to apply to a great majority of human beings. Language habits, acquired through everyday practice in speaking, ensure that in adulthood most people reach a level of fluency in their native language that allows them to use the language to get things done, without needing to reflect on the tool itself. Occasionally, we may become aware of our individual habits—our spelling difficulties, for instance, or the fact that we tend to use certain turns of phrase, which others may laugh at or fail to understand. *Collective habits*, patterns of speech attributable to a community, serve a particular purpose in that they help to define a group's identity; the protection of a language is then a means of safeguarding that identity. This can be seen to operate on a national and regional basis, in national languages and regional dialects, but it can also be observed on a smaller scale, in professional circles, and when friends or partners communicate in a way that only they can understand. Age and sex are often delimiting factors, so teenagers may have their own language, and men's language differs from women's (Swann 1992; Watson 1996).

The language variety that sets aside a community of speakers (e.g., computer specialists) is maintained thanks to their habits. On the downside, however, habit is the opposite of variety, and feeling very comfortable with one's habits may lead to a reluctance to practice variation. In many face-to-face situations, especially dealing with an "outsider," we are forced to adapt or choose our language to suit the other person; if we do not, we soon feel the consequences; we see that we are failing to communicate, or someone tells us so, or we experience a negative reaction. In written communication—a letter, a brochure—we may never know if we failed to put across an intended message. This is also true of the communication that takes place through the computer interface or through user documentation, unless there is a specific mechanism for eliciting feedback on the language as it is used or checking the effectiveness of the message being conveyed.

The most appropriate language variety in any situation is the one that helps to achieve a given purpose. When purpose was mentioned in chapter 1, examples included instruction and assistance. In this book, special consideration is also given to explanation, labeling, and abbreviation, as these are language functions used for purposes that can be identified in many different systems. The total range in language is much wider: pleading, defending, negotiating, demanding, endorsing, stipulating, amusing, impressing, pretending, misleading, evading, praising, to name but a few.

Language variety also depends on geography (e.g., North American and British English) and history (e.g., Old English and modern). Such varieties are relatively easy to identify. Personal features such as personality type and intelligence level are more difficult to discern in language and are less often used as indicators of variety.

Colloquial (Everyday) and Formal (Special) Varieties

The word *colloquial*, which means "conversational," describes everyday, informal language that contrasts with language used on special occasions.

Sometimes colloquial means "very relaxed" and is used in relation to colorful expressions such as "I put my foot in it," "That'll take him down a peg or two," and "Don't be soft!" These largely figurative phrases may be used to ease any tension in a given situation.

In contrast, special occasions may be formal ones, involving a setting away from the home—an administrative office, a political platform, a church, a hospital—and the language is less familiar. However, a person's work environment can be a formal setting, yet it is also familiar to that person and therefore not special. This can be a source of communication problems with others who are not part of that setting (e.g., visitors, customers or clients, users of computer systems). The problem can be partly explained by the fact that a significant proportion of the language used in these special settings is in written form or is derived from written form (for example, a discussion based around a contract, a specification, or other document), and as will be shown in chapter 7, spoken and written language are rather different.

The setting itself is not the only determiner of the formality of language. At work, people often use informal, colloquial phrases: "Right, let's get on with it"; "I don't know what's got into him—he nearly bit my head off"; "I'll be in touch," etc. In this setting, formal words sometimes have informal variants, such as "job spec," "perks" (benefits), to "clinch" a business deal. In computing, formal words can have colloquial synonyms (the meaning may not be identical), as in Table 1.

Beyond the level of words and phrases, there are forms associated with types of discourse. For instance, presentations, lectures, and speeches are formal varieties of discourse, with many conventional elements of vocabulary as well as structure. The concept of *register* is applicable here, as defined by the linguist M. A. K. Halliday (1978):

> The image of language as merely the direct reflection of subject matter is simplistic and unsound, as Malinowski pointed out fifty years ago; there is much more to it than that, and this is what the notion of register is all about.
>
> A register is a set of meanings that is appropriate to a particular function of language, together with the words and structures which express these meanings. (pp. 33, 195)

Halliday also gives us an excellent way of conceptualizing the difference between *dialect* and *register*: Dialect is a language variety "according to the user" (p. 35), that is, spoken habitually, determined by who the user is and expressing diversity of social structure; register, on the other hand, is a variety "according to the use"—the variety used in a particular circumstance, determined by one's activity, and expressing diversity of social process rather than of social hierarchy or structure. The term dialect, as used in computing, contrasts with both these meanings: "dialect = a version of a programming

Table 1. Formal words
with colloquial synonyms

Formal	Colloquial
requirement	need
advantage	plus
authority	right
edit	change
create	make
insert	put in
sufficient	enough

language that closely resembles other versions, but also differs in other respects" (Rosenberg 1987).

Formal language, or register, tends to favor abstract meanings, through words such as *procedure, method, type, extent, arrangement, control, global, comprehensive,* and *detailed.* But formal terms need not be abstract (e.g., *to view, to connect*), and abstract terms need not be formal (e.g., *change, steps*).

Colloquial expressions are frequently used in the table of contents and in the text of a user guide, setting a relaxed tone and giving the impression that concepts are accessible despite the technical language. At the same time, however, the index to the book typically does not contain this type of colloquial expression, so technical terms are needed for retrieval anyway (Box 12).

The Complete Idiot's Guide to the Internet (Kent 1994)

Some subsection headings from the table of contents:

Picking the Software You Need
Grabbing the Goodies—Downloading Files with FTP
Messing with Files
Now, Where's That Address?
Getting to Archie

Typical index entries for the same topic areas:

Dial-in terminal connections
Accessing FTP
File Transfer Protocol
Deleting files
Accessing archie

Box 12. Colloquial expressions and corresponding
technical terms

Going one step further, a type of figurative colloquial language may be used that is impractical for retrieval purposes, even in the table of contents (Box 13).

The main causes of this type of problem are the fact that in tables of contents, the dual purpose of headings, to attract the reader and to signal contents, has not been properly maintained, and in the case of the index, it is the widespread conservative approach to back-of-book indexing, based on the assumption that the index should or can only cover technical terms. Both types of access mechanisms provide an overview of contents, which ought to be tailored to prospective users. This normally implies making substantial changes both to the original headings, used to guide the writing process, and to the list of technical terms, compiled straight from the text.

General and Professional Varieties

When we think of the common distinction between general and specialist knowledge, we can appreciate that there is also a *general language*. This is a more neutral term than *colloquial language*, since the latter suggests casual chit-chat, whereas the label "general" is both wider and nonjudgmental.

In computing literature, *natural language* was originally used as a label to distinguish it from *artificial language*, but more recently a debate has developed concerning the desirability of "natural words" in human-computer interactions (Eberts 1994, pp. 56–58). This debate seems largely unhelpful because the word "natural" is very contentious in relation to language. Anyone interested in following this up from a language specialist point of view should read Sinclair (1984, 1991), who has written at length about "naturalness" in language. In the context of computing, the label "general" is certainly useful for talking about words such as *problem, range, time, level, central, control, check,* and *message*—words that are not specific to computing but are used a good deal in the domain. When finer distinctions are drawn, some of these words can be said to belong to scientific or technical language and to particular special subject languages. The label "general" is especially useful when we

---

Desktop Publishing with WordPerfect 5.0 (Tevis 1989)

From the table of contents:

Doing the Dirty Work
No Word Is an Island
WordPerfect Sure Is Nosy
Saving the Best for Last

Box 13. Figurative colloquial language

want to distinguish between various uses of words in different spheres of life (i.e., daily life versus a specialized activity), in order to draw attention to the differences; this would apply to words like *language, document, index,* and *character,* which are used in daily life and in professional contexts, but in different ways. Sometimes computing terms are words that are also used in other special subjects, and this can lead to confusion on the computer screen (e.g., *cancel* is used in computing and in algebra, so an application that teaches algebra would need to be careful about the use of this term).

Within a particular professional variety, one expects to find a range of terms and expressions being used regularly and consistently—this habitual use of terms and the patterns formed in discourse help to distinguish that variety from others. Consistency within a professional variety is especially important for communication. In interfaces and documentation, a lack of consistency with no adequate explanation can lead to confusion. This is not to say that varieties cannot be mixed in an interface, but it should be obvious to the user where one variety ends and another begins (e.g., different areas of the screen or manual, different use of presentation styles and colors).

For example, in Microsoft Works 3.0 "Startup Dialog," the words *document* (a business term) and *file* (meaning a computer file) both appear on the screen, but there are no clear boundaries to help the user. On this screen, a spreadsheet, for instance, can be a document and a file at the same time (Box 14).

The general language can serve to express lay, as opposed to professional, opinion. A letter to the editor of a newspaper from a member of the general public can be an example of lay opinion concerning a professional matter. Such a letter is likely to be written in a formal style, and this illustrates that "formal" does not necessarily equate with "professional" (Box 15). A doctor, a lawyer, or a computer specialist can give a professional opinion, information, advice, in either a formal or informal way.

"The vernacular" is a term that is now falling out of use, but for many years it meant "the phraseology of a profession or trade" (e.g., *the vernacular of*

New & Recent *Documents*

Choose a new *document* type or choose a *file* from the
Recently used *files* list.
   Create a new
   Word Processor   Spreadsheet   Database   Communications

Recently used *files*:
          \MSOFFICE\WINWORD\ABC.DOC
          \MSOFFICE\WINWORD\XYZ.DOC

Box 14. Part of Microsoft Works "Startup Dialog" document and file (emphasis added)

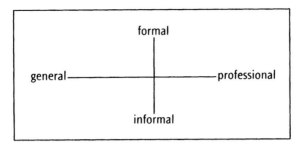

Box 15. Four language varieties

engineers (Shorter OED 1983); its original meaning was "the native language" (as distinct from Latin). "Phraseology" would be the phrases used by these people—their professional or trade language.

Scientific and Technical Language, Jargon, and Slang

For someone working in science or technology, scientific and technical language is their professional language. It reflects the mental and physical constructs of this broad area, ranging from ones that are highly abstract to those that are quite concrete, encompassing theories, principles, models, methods, techniques, processes, measures, objects, agents, substances, tools, and so on. It turns words that are in the general language (e.g., *problem, range, level*) into scientific and technical terms through more frequent and more precise usage.

The language of computing can have in it elements of both computer *science* and computer *technology*. Scientific terms would be ones such as *algorithm, command, field, branching, variable, string*; technology-oriented terms might be: *disk, terminal, memory, modem*, and so on. "Computing" as a global term implies an activity (processing, merging, swapping, saving, etc.) and can be regarded as an applied area of knowledge, but it is also used loosely as a general term. When it relates to administrative and organizational tasks, certain words come to the fore (e.g., *file, database, sort, log, audit*). The terms "information technology" and "information systems" again emphasize different aspects of computing.

What we are leading up to here is that it is not at all unusual to find words belonging to several different aspects of computing in one application. In addition, other domains of knowledge may be mixed in; for example, the domains of typography and editing within a word processing system. This makes for a terminological mish-mash, a lack of conceptual clarity, and sometimes a mixture of levels of abstraction. For example, in Microsoft Word 4.0 for Macintosh, a user should understand what *utilities* and *commands* are for; know what *file formats* are; be able to distinguish *footer* from *footnote*, *tab* from *indent*, *character styles* from *format styles*; understand what *gutters* are, and so forth. Anyone wishing to understand the area of computer security needs to be able to deal with the language of (Kukulska-Hulme 1993):

- abstract and scientific concepts (*strategy, analysis, probability*)
- technology (*voltage, pressure, circuitry, surge*)
- computing (*backup, write protect, system crash*)
- mathematics (*operand, factoring algorithm, primitive constant*)
- security (*risk, intrusion, protection, privacy, authorization*)
- computer security (*asynchronous attack, privileged user, deciphering*)
- business (*responsibility, audit, asset, scenario, policy*)
- law (*illegal, unlawful, apprehend, license, damages, compensation*)
- linguistics (*jargon, phonetic password, letter frequency in English*)

Advice often given to designers is that help and tutorial material "should be written in clear, familiar language, avoiding jargon as much as possible" (Dix et al. 1993, p. 417). But what exactly is *jargon*? To an uninitiated user, terms like the ones mentioned above come across as jargon. Jargon is essentially meaningless to those who are not part of the community of people who belong to a particular profession, trade, art, or science. It is not meaningless in itself, only to outsiders. In addition, very long, complex sentences in which such terms are sometimes embedded can make the language difficult even for those who are supposed to understand it.

As an outsider, you can try guessing the meanings of some jargon terms, whereas others are much more obscure. *Network, archive,* or *layout* may be computing terms, but they are less likely to be thought of as jargon than terms like *emulation, interleave, parallax,* or *parsing,* because the former will have been encountered in other contexts, yet all are examples of jargon because of their special meanings. Jargon typically contains highly specialized, technical terms and expressions, which may or may not look distinctive. It is not exactly the same as what is known as a *restricted language* (e.g., the language of sea navigation control, sports scores reporting, citizen band radio), where there are strict rules about the use of certain vocabulary items, sequences, and structures, and where a limited function is very clearly defined. In computing, "pseudocode" might be considered one example of a restricted language.

Jargon is at times indistinguishable from *slang*. Wales tells us that slang "is closer to argot or anti-language, in that standard lexical items are replaced by relexicalizations which are characteristically very informal, and designed, like a 'secret language,' to be unintelligible to the uninitiated." (*Argot* was originally the language of thieves and rogues.) "There is something of this 'in-group' or solidarity tendency in professional jargon," she continues "Slang is less socially 'acceptable' than jargon, and more socially subversive" (1989, p. 423).

A broader notion of slang includes "words and expressions that are ugly or overused" [entry for "slang" in Grimand (1986)]; for example, *the bottom line, guesstimate, option, major, key, massive, problem.* Here slang overlaps with the notion of a cliché or a hackneyed phrase (usually a phrase rather than a word).

In computing, there are many informal terms that are typically referred to as jargon but are also examples of a form of slang, such as the *look* and *feel* of a user interface, *sticky* menus, *hot* key, *pop-up* menu, *creeping featuritis, software bloat, pain in the net.*

International Communication in English

Variety, in the forms that we have considered here, is an inevitable and generally welcome feature of any language, but it can stand in the way of communication. Even the elusive concept of a neutral, *Standard English,* which has been explored by linguists, does not offer a solution to communication problems, first because it is very difficult to identify criteria for such a version of the language (Is it possible, as would be necessary, to ignore the social aspects of language?), and second, because English is an international language and so cannot have just one "standard." Milroy (1994) argues that "standardization is better interpreted dynamically as a *sociolinguistic process* than as a label which can reliably be attached to a particular variety of English" (p. 156).

In fact, English is so obviously made up of geographically determined varieties that some authors [e.g., Smith (1987)] speak of "Englishes," not "English." Trudgill and Hannah (1994), in their book *International English—A Guide to the Varieties of Standard English,* mention two "standard" varieties, British and North American, along with many others: South African, Welsh, Scottish, Irish, New Zealand, Australian, West Indian, West African, and Indian English.

It is so easy to suppose that other speakers of English will understand the words we use and will share our assumptions about meanings. Shared assumptions have been investigated by linguists and psychologists and have been given the name of *prototypes* of meaning. Aitchison (1994) provides a clear summary and discussion of the prototype theory first developed by Rosch (1975) and later extended by Lakoff (1987) and others. Prototypes of meaning are mental models carried around in the minds of native speakers of a language. Within one culture, there can be a great deal of commonality between the meaning prototypes of individual speakers, but cross-cultural comparisons reveal differences, such as "having a bath" in England and in India, where the actions and props are quite different (Aitchison 1994, p. 94), or taking tea, which might involve drinking a cup of tea, or might mean "high tea with scones," depending on where it is taken.

Nonnative speakers (indeed, all learners of a new language) are known to have problems with "false friends"—words that look or sound alike in two languages but have very different meanings (e.g., the French word *capitalisation* is only used in an economic sense). Another difficult area are formal and technical words that are not normally encountered in language-learning situations; for example, the meanings of word processing terms like *paste* and *merge* will be far from obvious to nonnative speakers, although in the same application they will readily understand terms like *repeat* or *replace*. Many nonnative users report bypassing meaning altogether, preferring instead to learn that a certain sequence of keys or an item in a given position in a menu performs the action they want and that they understand in their own language. If a new version of the software is released and differs from what they are accustomed to, they are unable to adapt as quickly as native speakers.

If the English language is in some sense "too rich" for effective communication, then one way of overcoming that problem might be to propose that the number of words and sentence rules presently in use should be reduced for a particular situation or group of people. In English language learning, such an approach was worked out in the 1930s and later refined (Ogden 1930, 1968; Richards 1943), and it is known by the name of *Basic English*. In the Basic English word list, there are three categories of words: things (e.g., *animal, attempt, stage*), qualities (e.g., *clear, public, special*) and "operations" (e.g., *see, have, between, than*). Carter (1987) gives a review of this topic and makes the interesting remark that "grammatical words are essential and ubiquitous in the basic communication uses of a language" (p. 27); examples of these grammatical words can be found in the "operations" category—*between, than, off, for, the, but*, and so on. For someone learning English, a limited vocabulary is quick and easy to assimilate; it is also surprisingly versatile. Delimiting English in this way does not solve the problem of multiple meanings in the general language, but in professional varieties this approach could make it more feasible to formulate definitions for words or to identify a set of uses for each word. This is relevant to interface and documentation design, since it is a device that could help the user.

Another approach to reducing the complexity of English in specific circumstances is embodied in the Plain English movements of Britain and the United States, which originated in the late 1970s and continue to have an impact today. The idea is to make certain that documents produced by governments, banks, lawyers, pharmaceutical companies, and the like are comprehensible to the public at large. Writing strategies recommended by the campaigners include avoidance of jargon, use of shorter words and sentences, use of verbs rather than nouns, using good punctuation, making documents visually appealing, and so on (Cutts and Maher 1986; Cutts 1996; Dayananda 1986). In deciding whether strategies of this type might be applicable to user interface design, one has to take into account the types and functions of texts being targeted by these campaigns: brochures, forms, instructions, product descriptions, and contracts. There is certainly plenty of overlap with the language of the user interface and documentation, but in an interactive computer environment the constraints and possibilities are not exactly the same.

Variety in Writing Style

Like the notion of slang, style is difficult to define, as it is not a precise concept. "Style" is sometimes used to refer to the different varieties of language encountered in different situations—so "informal variety" could be replaced with "informal style." It tends to be used in reference to writing rather than speaking. It is a largely intuitive concept, though elements of style can be described and measured just like other more tangible aspects of writing. Descriptions of style in a specific piece of writing often relate to the personality of the author as reflected in the writing (e.g., *somber, lively, pompous*), to the effect on readers (e.g., *persuasive, patronizing*), to the form and content of the writing itself (e.g., *telegraphic, administrative*).

Grimand (1986) equates style with "clarity of writing" and offers a number of miscellaneous general rules that help writers to achieve this:

- do not be stuffy or pompous,
- do not be hectoring or arrogant,
- keep complicated constructions and gimmicks to a minimum,
- do not be too chatty.

General rules are bound to attract many exceptions, and much depends on the audience or publication in question. We can pause to consider, for instance, whether a "chatty" style can be appropriate in a user guide. Krol's *The Whole Internet* (1994) has a chapter on dealing with problems, where these sentences may be found:

> "If you have changed anything, a file or some hardware thingy . . ."
> (p. 358)
> "I don't think you are dumb." (p. 352)

Words like *thingy* and *dumb* appear to have psychological purposes in this chapter: reassurance of the inexperienced but avoidance of insulting the knowledgeable. They also reflect the author's personal style of writing. To a reader more accustomed to British than American English, they present as a specifically American, laid-back writing style. American English is sometimes also perceived by speakers of British English as favoring more complicated ways of describing simple things. Certainly, the question of style becomes very relevant when communication across cultural lines is taking place. Compared with many other languages, English (in its many varieties) has more down-to-earth synonyms for words that sound "elevated" (e.g., *teacher* rather than *pedagogue*). Scollon and Scollon (1995) raises many issues connected with writing style, giving extensive coverage of the notion of politeness in intercultural communication systems and strategies.

The development of an author's capacity to write in different styles is part of the way in which one's language continues to change beyond the childhood and teenage years. Change in the language of adults, especially computer users, as well as change in language itself (including computing terminology), is the subject of the next chapter.

FOUR

Language Change

- Are computer applications changing our language?
- Why do some people reject technology?
- Are adults willing to change their language?
- Do other cultures want to borrow English computing terms?
- Is our knowledge of word meanings out of date?

In this chapter on language change, we address these questions first by examining the reasons for change and looking at the various types of change that can occur.

We then focus on developments in the language of adults (life-long language learning) and on how language is organized in the minds of speakers. We consider people's expectations with regard to meanings as well as the process of acquiring new words and meanings.

The final part of the chapter deals with the issue of borrowing words from other languages.

Motivations for Change

No one really knows why languages change over time, though a number of possible explanations have been put forward concerning specific instances of change. Historical events can sometimes provide explanations, when *new contact* or *loss of contact* between groups of people is eventually reflected in the word stock or sounds of a language. It is interesting to speculate whether electronic contact (e.g., through the Internet) might have the same degree of power to change languages over time. Certainly, in that environment, as in the "real world," social forces can be observed: Borrowing words from another language and integrating them into one's own can be part of a process of wanting to imitate another culture—especially one that is seen to be more fashionable or more technologically advanced.

If new objects, ideas, and processes have to be named, new words will appear; similarly, old ones will fall out of use. Technological advancements contribute to these needs. They also create *new human communication environments*, which require new forms of text or speech, which in turn have an effect on the language to be used. For instance, in electronic communication, punctuation and spelling may differ from what is expected in other media; some languages may operate in different scripts or without their usual accented characters; new forms of access to information or engagement in online debate may call for new language forms and graphic symbols, such as the smiling face on its side :-) as an example of an "emoticon"; and so on.

Having just looked at variation in language in the previous chapter, we can start to see how language change is something that might occur in just one language variety, or it might start there and then spread to others. There is nothing regular or entirely predictable about change. It is initiated by individuals of all ages, though the younger generation appears to play a more significant role. It is diffused by groups of people and may end up being sanctioned by some form of authority within a community of speakers. An authority can sometimes initiate change in line with a language policy.

When abbreviated forms are used in place of longer phrases, as so often happens in computing, e.g., *RAM*, *DOS*, and *ID*, it is reasonable to suppose that *speed* and *improved efficiency of communication* are the reasons. Loss of transparency of meaning may well be the by-product of such change, when abbreviations are not widely known, for instance because they are specific to a manufacturer, e.g., Apple Desktop Bus (*ADB*). At other times, the shorter version successfully hides the complexity of meaning from casual users (e.g., *modem*).

Some aspects of language change, such as the pronunciation of words, can take many years to evolve, whereas others—such as the appearance of new words—can be observed over a period of just a few days, weeks, or months. In computing, the rate of change is very high, and some words have, in language terms, a relatively short active life span (e.g., *punch card*). Languages generally appear to have a tendency toward regularity, so that some changes seem to occur to bring certain forms into line with rules in the language (e.g., "cows" has replaced the earlier "kine" as the plural form of "cow" (Fromkin and Rodman 1993, p. 349).

Change can also be related to an individual person, whose vocabulary, accent, and so on undergo changes over the course of a lifetime, perhaps in line with the development of personal relationships and career. Some of those changes will be attributable to changes going on in the language varieties in which the person participates, whereas others will be down to personal choices (conscious or unconscious, often socially conditioned); such as in vocabulary, a preference for *television* over *TV*. Choices can be dictated by personal goals, such as the need to identify with a group, or to become more "visible" in one's professional territory by forging a distinct set of terms reflecting one's particular point of view.

For the individual person, the fast rate of change in computing terminology requires constant adaptation. People who are not able to adapt their language quickly may eventually reject the technology. As the user interface is so often the *instigator* of language change in the individual user, and through that user in a wider group, it is up to interface designers to take on the responsibility of thinking through the implications of that process before making decisions about the language aspects of an application. At the same time, the user interface should itself be adaptable and *allow* for language change within reasonable constraints.

Types of Change in the Language

Looking more closely at what types of change occur in a language, we can say that the language evolves at different levels: sound, meaning, structure, and so on. Languages that are geographical neighbors interact with each other and this brings about modifications (it can happen in neighboring countries or through the languages of immigrants), but they also evolve through other types of grouping—for instance, languages whose speakers are involved in new technology developments. A *dominant language* might then impose itself on others, as is currently happening with English in information technology. In much the same vein, a language variety (e.g., the language of computing) can spill over into the general language. Sound changes occur in the language when sounds merge, split, change places, and when they are lost or added. As noted earlier, however, sound changes tend to be slow compared with changes in vocabulary.

New words can be easy to spot: They may be borrowed from another language, so they stand out in their new surroundings. They may be abbreviations or acronyms, which perhaps stand out because of their capital letters, or brand names, made conspicuous by advertising. We tend to notice less the broadening or narrowing of meanings, as in *navigation* (seacraft only at first, then aircraft, now software) and might not even consider such words to be new. Shifts in meaning (e.g., *naughty* used to mean "worth noting") can be gradual, so that speakers are not aware of them taking place. Changes in spelling (e.g., *aeroplane, airplane*) may fail to register as changes. Variations in spelling (e.g., in computing: *sign-on, signon; back-up, backup; id, ID*) can be symptoms of transition, as new meanings try to establish themselves.

Another type of language change occurs when certain words come to be used more frequently, as they become fashionable or necessary. The word *hot* is currently being added to or used with computing terms in a productive way; such as in *hot plugging, hotkey, hot spot*. A word beginning (prefix) or ending (suffix) can become "productive" when added to many words or when words with those elements are used frequently. The prefix "un-" is a recent example of this in computing (*undelete, unnest, unsend*); the suffixes "-ize" and "-ware" are currently highly productive (*customize, personalize, capitalize, alphabetize, optimize; shareware, payware, vapourware, freeware, guiltware*). Anyone wishing to study language change in greater depth will benefit from consulting Halliday (1978, p. 195), where a brief but systematic description of the development of the vocabulary of mathematics may be found (the various categories of innovation and change it mentions can be applied to other subject areas).

Does it matter whether we can recognize words or parts of words as being new? As users, we may have incomplete knowledge of meanings and possible word forms, which can lead to incorrect interpretation of messages and to frustration in access or retrieval. As designers and authors, if we do not know we are dealing with new elements, we will treat them like old ones and ignore the needs of users.

The emergence of new terms in a specialized subject field has been referred to as "terminology-in-the-making" (Pavel 1993). Descriptive phrases and *neologisms*—terms with a "new" status—are as much a part of it as terms created on the spot and immediately accepted into usage (the latter is in fact unusual). It is this dynamic nature of terminologies, and particularly computing terminology, which makes the design of the language interface such a challenging task. Emerging terminologies can be observed with reference to the Internet and the World Wide Web (Box 16). Many educational Web sites make use of terms whose meaning has to be reinterpreted in that setting, such as *course, textbook, seminar*. Normal assumptions about form, duration, people involved, and so on, do not apply in the case of virtual learning, but this is often implicit rather than explicit. Expressions like *on-line course* or *interactive textbook* can be helpful in establishing a distinction. Web sites also tend to present a new image of familiar objects or institutions. For example, to many people, a *museum* is a place that puts on *exhibitions*, yet the fact that museums also have *collections* that are not exhibited is less well known. A museum Web site that offers these two links (*exhibitions, collections*) is offering a choice that may not be immediately understood if no explanation is given.

Change in the Individual: Adult Language Development

As we know, children do not learn to speak a language overnight. Instead, there are stages to go through, and with each stage the child comes closer to speaking like an adult. When that goal has been reached, however, it is not the end

Some phrases that have emerged as single terms:

a program for reading hypertext, for browsing . . . . *browser*
a list of Web sites that you find interesting . . . . *hotlist,   bookmarks*
an aggressive personal attack in a newsgroup . . . . *flame*

Some phrases that may emerge as single terms:

- documents generated "on the fly"
- links to public documents
- a link that you have visited before
- an integrated browser and editor
- a hypertext editor for collaborative work
- to turn cross-references into links
- to follow several different search paths

Box 16. Emerging terminologies: use of the Internet and the World Wide Web

of the journey. We normally continue to widen and alter our knowledge of our language throughout our lives—thus language learning is a lifelong enterprise. Few adults set out to deliberately change their language, but circumstances can bring this about. Besides, there is pleasure to be had from learning new words, through reading, word puzzles, or games, for instance. There is also a growth in confidence: confidence in the use of new words as well as in their understanding. Some people choose to learn a second language (or more) for the express personal motives of pleasure and confidence. Learning another language also helps to better understand one's own, through the intellectual process of comparison that is repeatedly activated in that learning situation.

A different kind of motive is a need connected to communication. We may learn foreign languages, professional or stylistic varieties for that reason. *Maintaining communication* might be an end in itself, or a step toward getting something done—language as a tool for action. Although it may seem surprising, a person using a computer system is in a language learning situation. In the frontmatter of the *Longman Language Activator* dictionary (Summers 1993), Paul Meara explains one important aspect of the process of foreign vocabulary acquisition (e.g., someone learning to speak English), which will serve to illustrate this point when applied to the computer environment:

When you pick up a word from reading, you have a general idea of what it means, without being clear about the detailed meaning of the new word, and, more importantly, how it can be used.
Suppose for example, that you learn the word *burgle* from watching a movie on TV. You know that it has something to do with stealing

things from somewhere. That might be all you need to know if you are watching a film, but it's easy to make the wrong inferences about words like this. For instance, can you *burgle* a person, or somebody's wallet? Can you *burgle* an idea? If you take something from a shop without paying for it, have you *burgled*? What exactly is the difference between *burgle*, and other words you might know with a similar meaning like *shoplift, loot, pinch, mug, embezzle, hold up* and so on? (p. F15)

In a computer environment, if I am able to *demote* a heading in a document outline, I know that this word is used to mean "moving something to a lower level." Is it also appropriate for me to use *demote* when I want to find out, through on-line help or a manual, how to move a file to a lower level in a directory?

Conversely, the user may only know the general concept ("moving something to a lower level"), but not have any specific term in mind. In information systems, education, or training applications, a user may "want to know" something, and "need to ask some questions." The next stage is knowing that this translates into *formulating* a *query* and *searching* for information in a *database*, perhaps even *creating a refined* search. A change of language thus precedes and is a condition of the ability to see results from an application. On the positive side, through language, users can start to appropriate an application. If the interface is favorable in that respect, users will *feel able to allow their language to change.* They may also want to have the option of changing the language on the screen; in some personal applications, this is feasible. Letting users vote on the names of features in an interface at the design stage, based on a short list of possible choices, can be a particularly successful strategy (Bloom 1987–1988). Nielsen (1993) mentions this approach and emphasizes that vote-winning terms enabled users "to understand the system better in that they could generalize their knowledge to correctly use it in new ways" (1993, p. 126). Foster (1994), Howard et al. (1991) and Rogers and Osborne (1987) make similar suggestions with regard to choosing symbols.

Repertoires of Words, Terms, and Structures

The changes that occur in a language are recorded in two places: in *the minds of speakers* and in *repositories of writing and speech.* The latter may be transient or more enduring writings and recordings. Typically, their main function will not be the registering of language change—that will be an implicit role they play. The most systematic ones, such as dictionaries and other reference works, may be designed specifically for noting change; for instance, dictionaries of new words. When learning a new language, people sometimes use a notebook or a more structured database to keep track of the words they are learning. These cumulative vocabulary lists are an aid to memory and a visible record of the fact that their new language is changing. They are a temporary written record in the journey of a vocabulary item from its original context of use to potential new contexts—from understanding to productive use (Kukulska-Hulme 1988a). Dictionaries for language learners are sometimes now organized specifically with the aim of helping their users to speak and write, rather than to just understand—Summers (1993) mentioned earlier is an example of such a tool for learners of English.

If we look at the language of the user interface to any system in that light, we can see that it might serve a similar function. The user must go through the stages of 1. understanding the language and 2. moving on to a stage of being able to use it actively to carry out particular goals (e.g., searching, calculating, organizing). In the analogy, the first context is the designer's view of the application ("these are the available functions, and this is how they have been named"), the second, the productive one, is the user's view ("which name do I use to achieve my goal?").

As well as understanding individual "names," for productive purposes the user should be able to see how the whole repertoire is organized. In everyday life, we all have repertoires of words and terms for the various activities we engage in. These repertoires can be activated when needed. We also have the ability to activate language structures, so that we can construct meaningful words, phrases, and sentences. Words in the mind "seem to be organized in semantic fields, and within these fields there are strong bonds between coordinates which share the same word class" (Aitchison 1987, p. 191). Put another way, words that are related in meaning, on the same level of detail, and belonging to the same grammatical category, seem to be grouped together (e.g., *bread* with *butter; red* with *black, white, blue,* and *green; rain* with *snow,* and so on). Aitchison points out that there are also links between "collocates" (words that are often used together), such as *bright* with *red*; links to superordinates, such as *red, color*; and links between synonyms, such as *hungry, starved.*

The semantic organization of the mental lexicon (mental dictionary) appears to be geared towards speech *production* rather than *comprehension.* Much more is known about how the mental lexicon is structured from word association experiments. Indeed, there is a considerable body of research in this area in relation to the general language, but more work could be done on the organization of the mental lexicon of computing terms to explore it in a similar way. The interesting point here is that human language is first learned through speech, enriched through reading, and used predominantly in speech, whereas computing terminology might first be encountered in written form and for the most part used in that form—of course, it will depend on the terms themselves, on the user, and on the application.

Prior Knowledge of Words and Terms

If we accept that there is an ongoing process of change in a language, particularly in its lexical component, then any previous knowledge of word meanings and uses that a person has is potentially out of date. In this sense, all knowledge of meanings is "prior" knowledge, but of course it is not necessarily outdated in any significant way. The mental lexicon is not organized in a neat and tidy fashion, in the sense that prior or background knowledge may consist of various associations, not all of which are helpful at the time when a word is to be understood or used. This might happen when the words in question are not part of a person's habitual repertoire. For instance, knowledge of the meaning of specialized terms that originate from or resemble words in the general language may have in it elements of the general language meaning [see Kukulska-Hulme (1990a) for a discussion of the data communications terms *alert*, *event* and *focal point* in this light]. To a new user of an application, what does an option that reads *Find Entry* offer? The application context (e.g., a glossary) gives one clue as to what might be meant by "entry," but this assumes that users will pick up that clue, which in turn presupposes that they are aware at all times which application (module, system, etc.) is currently running or being displayed, so that language can be interpreted in its intended task-related context.

In other cases, where similar terms are used in different subject fields (e.g., chemistry and computing), *interference* may occur. For instance, what exactly happens when you "activate" something? It depends on the subject field (and then also on the particular objects within the field). As computer users move between systems and applications, the different ways the same terms have apparently been used can lead to confusion. Similar concepts are also designated by different terms (e.g., *contents* versus *overview*, *open* versus *retrieve*, *cancel* versus *undo*, *selecting text* versus *blocking text* or *highlighting text*). This is an important reason why there needs to be an explanation of the meanings of terms in any off-the-shelf application or in any application that replaces an earlier system (not necessarily computerized), even if within the perimeter of that application the meanings seem self-evident to its designers and are used consistently and with clarity.

Prior knowledge engenders expectations or assumptions about meanings. We can be sure or not so sure, right or not quite right about what we already know about a word. When we hear the word "broken," we might assume that something was previously in one piece, but without context we could be ruling out broken radios, coastlines, and promises, where the "one piece" assumption does not apply. In computing, if something is "locked," can we suppose it is inaccessible? For instance, can one *copy* information from a *locked* disk or file?

The information on a locked floppy disk, or in a locked file,
can be opened or copied but cannot be changed

states the *Macintosh User's Guide for PowerBook Computers* (Apple Computer Inc. 1992, p. 114). So it seems that information can be *opened* or *copied* while the disk or file remains *locked*. This may not accord with a user's prior knowledge of what it means for something to be locked.

In the Internet environment, browsing software can allow you to *open* a location. In this instance, "open" means "visit a new document specified by URL" [from a description of the Mosaic browser by Krol (1994)]. The meaning of "open" changes as one moves from one application environment to another.

Acquisition of New Terms: The Process

Prior knowledge of words and terms, as outlined above, is the unstable and imperfect foundation on which new knowledge is built. It plays a part in the mental models formed in the minds of users. It is worth noting that "chaotic and misconceived conceptual models are not merely an issue of 'early learning' and something that users outgrow. Experienced users hold them as well" (Carroll and Olson 1990, p. 54).

When computer users first encounter terms in a manual or on a computer screen, the sound component is usually missing. Conversely, if terms are encountered through the spoken medium (e.g., telephone support, training course), there is no immediate association with the word's form and hence its spelling. This has implications for memorization and for retrieval from memory, but the relationship is not simple. It has been shown that "orthographic priming" can assist retrieval from memory (Bowles and Poon 1985); so, for instance, knowing what letter a word begins with makes the word easier to recall. But different words with similar beginnings can designate a similar concept, so we must consider the possibility of the wrong word being retrieved from memory. To take the example of widely used word processing terminology, the word pairs *footer* and *footnote*, *border* and *box*, *form* and *format* are orthographically related and they also sound somewhat similar. If we hear the term *border* in a training video, for instance, and later go to use the application and see the term *box* in a menu, we might confuse it with *border* and then wonder why we cannot do what we intended. In other types of application, the terms to *clear* and to *close* can lead to confusion— their meanings and forms are similar. Special attention must be paid to these sets of terms in the design of any user interface (Box 17). If names cannot be changed, then ways of flagging the differences must be found (e.g., through cross-referencing, contextualization, or clear explanations).

What we are looking for here are ways of making up for incomplete knowledge on the part of the user, ways of speeding up the user's knowledge building by making explicit the connections that will eventually have to be made. It is useful to distinguish between partial knowledge (i.e., *incomplete but correct*) and knowledge that is *approximate and vague*, to the extent that the user

clear	close
expand	extend
refresh	restore
border	box
footer	footnote
header	heading
form	format
delete	demote
drop	drag
combine	condense
mark	bookmark

Box 17. Possible confusion
between terms of similar
form and meaning

misunderstands the meanings of terms. It is reasonable for the user to have incomplete knowledge: For instance, a process or system function may involve
various stages, and the user may not know what each stage entails. In this case,
as designers we would want to provide the information that these stages exist,
so that the empty knowledge "slots" can be filled in by the user in due course.

As computer users, we try to fit what we know into our mental representations of terms and concepts, our knowledge of the behavior and properties
of the objects we are dealing with in an application, the extent of our control
over those objects, the possible effects of our actions, and the wider scheme
of procedures, actions, and events that are admissible within the application.
We try to increase our understanding and confidence.

The process of acquisition of new terms can therefore be viewed as an initial phase of *contact* with the new term, becoming aware of its existence through
a particular medium, a second phase of fitting the term into one's knowledge
structures (*understanding*), and a third phase that involves *personal experience*
with the term: the experience of recognizing it when we come across it again
in similar or in new contexts and the experience of using the term. Of course,
the first contact can also be viewed as an experience of the term. A cycle then
emerges: from experience, to understanding, back to experience, and so on.

For people who are learning English, first contact with a new term in an application interface brings with it the added risk of misunderstanding based on
mispronunciation or confusion with a similar term in their mother tongue.

Borrowings: A Cultural Perspective

So far in this chapter we have been looking at the process of change in language as a whole and in individual speakers. Information technology is cur-

rently one of the main sources of language change. People whose language is directly affected will inevitably have various feelings about it. One attitude worth considering is the anxiety on the part of some users in the international community that English, particularly American English, is imposing itself on other languages by being the language of the front-runners in the technological race. The linguistic issue is that of *borrowings*—to what extent can one language borrow terms from another and still preserve its own identity. It is also a question of whether speakers feel that their language is being threatened. According to one estimate, of the 20,000 or so words in common use in English, about three-fifths are borrowed from other languages (Fromkin and Rodman 1993, p. 333), yet English speakers tend not to worry about borrowings. For English speakers outside of the American continents, an "American accent," which is a feature of the language in many commercial multimedia packages available worldwide, tends to be noticed before any other language qualities and may be a source of disquiet. Spelling differences are also a source of concern in educational settings.

In computing terminology, we are chiefly dealing with other languages that borrow whole words from American or British English; the borrowing of parts of words is of less relevance in this particular sphere. However, changes are often made to an English word to make it fit into the other language. Phonetic (sound) integration is the top priority, so an English word may change its spelling to make it easier to pronounce; other changes include the introduction of gender or other alterations to make the word comply with various rules of grammar.

Borrowing is sometimes undertaken with a view to replacing the borrowed word in the longer term, but once a word has taken root in usage, it is difficult or impossible to replace. If an object has been borrowed together with its name, the connection between object and term is hard to break. It is also hard to break language habits, because, as we have seen earlier, they are there for a purpose. Language is embedded in culture, and terms are part of their special culture (e.g., computing or information technology).

One strategy for controlling borrowing is to have a language planning and protection policy. This is a high-priority area in some countries, and some have engaged in such activities for a long time. The traditional media (press, TV, radio) have in the past, with a few exceptions, been the preserve of prescriptive, protective values and attitudes to language that seem outdated now. The power of broadcasting and advertising exerts its influence on language more than ever. New media are both giving rise to changes in language and helping to spread them at a remarkable rate.

Although these wider issues have a bearing on what goes on in a particular company or establishment where system development is taking place, it is important to consider the matter at development level too. It is possible both to plan the terminological side of the user interface and to protect that terminology by specifying the meanings of each term, to encourage clarity and consistency of meaning within and across applications. A reliable and realistic mechanism for capturing terms and meanings and for communicating them within a team working on the design of an application is necessary. Definitions are not always the best way of capturing meanings. Chapter 6 throws light on this; definitions are also investigated in more depth in chapter 9.

But first we must look at the challenging problem of establishing equivalence between words, for that is a very important issue in definitions. The next chapter explores the concept of equivalence, and more broadly, the idea of "correspondence" between words in one or more languages.

FIVE

Language Correspondences

- Is a crossword puzzle clue a definition of a word?
- Can you enter to exit?
- Are unrecoverable errors recoverable?
- How can a word like "caution" mean "guarantee"?
- What is it that happens unless you do something else?

This chapter is about the ways in which elements of language are at times able to correspond to each other in usage and in meaning. It explains *equivalence*, the baseline for distinctions between words, and clarifies widespread misconceptions about *synonyms*. It shows that words have *values* that are sometimes obvious and sometimes concealed.

These concepts are relevant to all word choices in language, and they must be considered with due attention with *translation* of a user interface or documentation into another language. *Ambiguity* and *culture* are the two big issues that will inevitably come to the fore at such a time. It will also become clear that there are *gaps to be filled* in languages, and that *interference* and *confusion* are bound to get in the way. *Multiple language environments* create their own special demands with respect to all of these concepts.

Equivalence Between Words: Does It Exist?

In a typical crossword puzzle, we are asked to think of words that correspond to descriptions or suggestions of their meaning. Because a crossword is a kind of game, the clues may well be phrased so as to make the word discovery difficult. By contrast, in dictionaries, descriptions of meaning are meant to correspond much more directly to designated words. A direct link is made between a particular language element—a word or phrase—and the language used to express its meaning, which stands in or substitutes for that element in a variety of ways. Definition is one way, within one language; translation is another way, between languages. *Equivalence*, in the sense of a perfect match on the level of *meaning*, may be achieved through definition, which draws on a rich range of language resources. but equivalence is much more problematic in translation. In translation into a target language, a word with exactly the same meaning may not exist. If we then put this process of substitution into its proper context, description or translation of *usage*, a definition will have to describe or show how the word is used in various contexts. A translation will have to take usage into account when the choice of a word is made. Equivalence in both meaning and usage can be very difficult to achieve. Certain expressions of time, such as *occasionally* = *from time to time*, are given as rare examples of equivalence.

In computing, we have to look at whether established ways of describing meaning and using the notion of equivalence are adequate. On the face of it, *open* may not seem to be equivalent to *restore*, but *opening* a window in one computer environment may turn out to be an equivalent action to *restoring* a window in another environment. *Reducing* something to an icon may actually be the same as *closing* it elsewhere. *Dragging* might have the same effect as *copying*. This then raises the question of how we present such an action to a user. Is there a need to explain "self-evident" operations like *open* and *restore*, *reduce* and *close*, and *drag* and *copy*?

If we decide there is a need for it, because these terms are not self-evident, we must examine our options in terms of possible explanations. Let us take *open* and *restore* as an example. Do we explain *open* by reference to synonyms like *make visible, pull out, begin, expand*—which one might find in a thesaurus—and *restore* by reference to *rebuild, refresh, go back to, renew*? There is a danger that some of the more technical synonyms like *expand* and *refresh* will already be used in this or other applications. The everyday synonyms would be better for this purpose. But are they enough in themselves? Chapter 9 will address this question more fully. The point we need to make here is that we could also use *open* and *restore* as equivalents in an explanation (using one to stand in for the other), if we could establish that they have exactly the same meaning in a number of different applications or environments. But this assumes an expert knowledge of those other settings, and could introduce an element of confusion for some users. Explicit reference to one other named application is one solution to this problem, when users are experts in their use (Microsoft Word 6.0 for Windows does this for users of WordPerfect).

Sager (1994) specifically cites different approaches to equivalence in the field of translation; for instance, equivalence as a comparison of adequacy in relation to purpose, and "dynamic equivalence," which is on the level of a receptor's response and may be used as a kind of measure of success—the response to a successful translation hopefully being the same as the response to the original text. Other criteria applied in the translation field are "fidelity" to the original, "intelligibility" to end users (degree of clarity, reading time required), and "acceptability" of a text to its readers (in terms of the previous criteria, plus practical issues of usefulness, cost, and time delay). A coursebook on translation by Baker (1992) explores the concept of equivalence from every conceivable angle.

Synonyms and the Values of Words

Misconceptions about synonyms abound. Synonyms are commonly thought to be:

1. words with the same meaning (in fact, their meanings are similar and only rarely the same)
2. interchangeable within a sentence, without affecting the meaning of the sentence (but meaning is usually altered in some way)
3. helpful in information searches (this often depends on one knowing or recognizing the potential synonyms).

The concept of usage is again very relevant in trying to determine the extent of similarity between specific words. *Guess, surmise*, and *have a hunch* are similar, but the main difference here has to do with register (language level). In other cases, the difference is in the intensity of feeling expressed through each of the words, for instance, *painful* and *excruciating.*

When language variety or intensity do not apply, it can be difficult to distinguish between synonyms. For instance, some computer applications make reference to the ENTER and RETURN keys, to EXIT and QUIT. Are these considered pairs of equivalents (exactly the same) or are they synonyms (similar)? How will the user know? The user should not have to make that decision; it is up to the designer to think about the implications of using two words that refer to the same or similar object or action.

The language surrounding words like ENTER (names of keys) is unlikely to be helpful in establishing possible differences, such as *press* ENTER *to quit* on one screen and *press* RETURN *to quit* on another. The implication is that it is best either to eliminate synonyms or to show and explain the correspondences between them in a visible manner. An interesting case of the use of ENTER is the phrase:

Press ENTER *to* EXIT *help*

In everyday English, *enter* and *exit* are opposites (*antonyms*). The juxtaposition of these opposites is potentially confusing to a complete novice (Can one enter to exit?). In the Microsoft Windows 95 interface, one has to click the *Start* button to *shut down* the computer—*start* and *shut down* are antonyms.

In any windows environment, *minimize* and *close* are similar concepts; *notepads, wordpads,* and *clipboards* are similar. Between different systems and applications, there are many instances where synonyms are used for very similar concepts. For example, in various document handling and word processing systems, there are different terms for "notes added to a text":

> *annotations, attached notes, comments, hidden text, marginal notes, stickies*

Synonymy and antonymy are but two types of relations; in the field of lexical semantics, many more types have been noted, including various hierarchical relationships, semantic fields, logical categories of identity, inclusion, overlap and disjunction, syntagmatic relations such as tautonymy (redundancy), and others (Cruse 1986). There are also established methods of analyzing the components of meaning for comparative purposes. When we have to choose between a number of synonymous words in a foreign language, it may be necessary to do a more or less structured analysis of their differences [e.g., "to bring" in English can correspond to the French verbs "apporter" (to bring a thing), "amener" (to bring an animal), "faire venir" (to bring a person)].

A more elusive criterion for distinguishing between similar words is their *value*. In one interpretation, a word's value is the same as its meaning and usage. Baker (1992) tells us that the lexical meaning of a word "may be thought of as the specific value it has in a particular linguistic system and the 'personality' it acquires through usage within that system" (p. 12). In chapter 1, the communicative, convenience, and aesthetic values of language were mentioned, and these are obviously reflected in individual words. However, a word's value can also be interpreted as its *expressive, evaluative* meaning, as used by Cruse (1986). To take what might be considered an obvious example, the word *famous* is positive in its evaluation of a person, while *infamous* is negative. One's subjective perception may sometimes differ from the accepted norm; for a certain number of people, *infamous* will be positive, *famous* negative. Is *therapy* a positive word? Reactions are likely to differ, but within a particular social group or culture there may well be a concensus as to the value of given words. What about *fatal* and *illegal?* Nielsen (1993, p. 149) remarks that in good error messages, one should avoid such "abusive" terms.

Serious and *unrecoverable* are further examples of words to be used advisedly. A disk error described in these terms may indeed be serious from a processing point of view (e.g., an unformatted disk that cannot be written to), but a user can be unnecessarily alarmed by such terms. (The solution here may be simple: format the disk.) Error messages sometimes contain words like *unexpected* and *failed*, which are ambivalent in nature: If an error message says something was unexpected, does it imply the user should have foreseen it? If something failed, who is to blame? Users can also react badly to being told in an error message that something *does not exist*, when it is not an object's existence that is in question, but rather its location or accurate name, whether it can be *found*. Punctuation can change a word's value, such as *error!* compared with *error*—the two are not equivalent.

Users of educational and tutorial software may prefer to get a *prompt* or a *hint* rather than *help* from a computer, as there is a certain stigma attached to getting help, especially if someone else is watching (see also chapter 9 on the choice of words for psychological support). Children or people lacking in confidence will be particularly sensitive to these terms. However, terms like *prompt payment, prompt delivery* suggest something to be done at once, so the connotations of *prompt* may cause anxiety or confusion in some applications.

It is interesting to note that an expert verbally explaining his or her subject will use *value words* like *fatal, serious, dangerous,* and *undesirable,* and *belief words* like *possible, probable, likely,* and *certain* (Hart 1989). Written texts are more definitive in nature—they strive to freeze the results of experiment, experience, and thinking—so belief words are less likely to figure than in the expert's spoken language. The disparity between speech and text in this matter is particularly visible in texts of an explanatory or instructional nature, where the author must not be seen to waver. Both value words and belief words are also a feature of the nonspecialist's thinking and questioning in an unfamiliar subject area.

Interference and Confusion

In an earlier section on prior knowledge of terms, we mentioned that in cases where similar terms are used in different subject fields, interference can occur (for instance, what happens when you "activate" something?). We also said that, as computer users move between different systems and applications, the different ways in which terms have been used can lead to confusion. *Interference* tends to be associated with prior (historical) knowledge getting in the way of proper use and understanding, whereas *confusion* is generally discussed with reference to juxtapositions of words in the present.

Interference can occur on the level of form or meaning. The fact that children use *discover* where they should say *invent* and *invent* where they should say *discover* can be attributed to interference on the level of meaning—they are perhaps more confident about one of these words than the other, having had more prior experience of it, and not having noted the difference. Interfering "false friends" are a common problem between cognate (related) languages and cause difficulties for speakers of one language trying to learn and use the other. English and French share many words of Greek or Latin origin whose meanings have evolved differently over time, which can cause interference. In French, *report* means postponement, image transfer, amount carried forward; *agenda* can mean a calendar or a diary; *caution* is a security or a guarantee. It is so easy to assume quite wrongly that the same (or similar) form expresses the same meaning as the one we are familiar with in our first or native language. It is a treacherous area. [See Batchelor and Offord (1993) for an exhaustive practical account of misleading aspects of vocabulary in the French language as a whole; see also "Filling Gaps in a Language" in this chapter]. As another example, the English word *valid* is *valide* in French—but also *valable*, depending on context. There is a chance that native French-speaking users may experience interference when they come across English words that are similar to French words with different meanings (or even borrowed French words, like *repertoire*, which may be subtly different in meaning and usage!). This is especially likely out of context or when there is insufficient context (Box 18).

"English may be the universal language of software, but unless developers design products which work in the native language of the countries they're selling to, users will not give the packages a second glance" (Langley 1996, p. 20). To be successful, software firms need to localize their products, and translation tools can be used for that purpose, but neither human nor computer-assisted translation is a simple process. If designers and technical authors are aware of the difficulties involved, some of them can be avoided. Langley does indeed go on to say that "translation stands a better chance of success if source texts, such as manuals, are written with translation in mind." Anyone wishing to gain an insight into the process of translation should be in touch with professional translators who can explain how they go about their work. Books

report	"postponement, image transfer, amount carried forward"
agenda	"diary"
caution	"security, guarantee"
trouble	"agitation, confusion"
venue	"arrival"
stage	"training period"
trivial	"vulgar, commonplace"
phrase	"sentence"

replace looks similar to the French *replacer*, which means "to put back again" (*remplacer* is "to put something in the place of something else")

ignore looks similar to *ignorer*, which means "to not know"

delay looks similar to *délai*, which means "time allowed"

actual looks similar to *actuel*, which means "present, current"

eventual looks similar to *éventuel*, which means "possible"

Box 18. Potential false friends in user interfaces—English and French on the subject include Bell (1991) and Larson (1984), the second of these being a much more substantial tome than the first. Microsoft Corp. (1995) includes a section on internationalization and contains some very general, basic guidelines on the translation of text.

It is also worth bearing in mind that many nonnative speakers will be using English language software because they are with a company whose employees work in the medium of English, regardless of location. In other situations, nonnative speakers are the people who evaluate demonstration software and make purchasing decisions before translation takes place. There is a strong argument here for making a user interface appeal to both native and nonnative speakers. Table 2 gives examples of Portuguese, Spanish, Italian, and French terms that resemble English terms—but don't correspond to! For instance, the Italian *cancellare* corresponds in meaning to the English *delete*, though in form it is more like *cancel*, which could be confusing for Italian speakers using English language software.

In English, confusion can occur between words that are similar (e.g., *junction* and *juncture*, *footer* and *footnote*). Sometimes known as *confusibles*, these words have a similar sound and spelling and are linked in meaning. In more traditional linguistic terminology, a confusing word that is derived from another, or has the same root, is known as a *paronym*. As a further distinction, Room (1985) uses the label *distinguishables* for words that are unlike each other in sound or spelling but are closely related in meaning (e.g., *mistake*, *error*, and *fault*; *magazine* and *journal*). Essentially these are synonyms that are often used incorrectly.

Table 2. English terms in relation to other languages: confusing similarities

English	Portuguese	Spanish	Italian	French	Similar to
delete (v.)			cancellare		cancel
file (n.)	arquivo				archive
remove (v.)		quitar			quit
string (n.)	fileira	serie		chaine	file, series, chain
row (n.)	fila	fila	fila	ligne	file, line
log (n.)	diário	registro	registro		diary, register
output (v.)		extraer		sortir	extract, sort
sort (v.)	classificar	clasificar	classificare		classify
sort (n.)		clasificación	selezione		classification, selection
record (n.)	registo	registro		article	register, article
lock out (v.)	bloquear	bloquear		bloquer	block
relocate (v.)				translater	translate
crash (n.)				accélération	acceleration
bug (n.)				défaut	default
address (n.)		dirección			direction
directory (n.)				répertoire	repertoire

Source: Isaacs (1981) with additional examples from other sources.

For nonnative speakers or learners of English, it is perhaps the area of *phrasal verbs* that is the most confusing. What prepositions can one attach to verbs like *take* or *put* in English? *Take in, take on, take off, take out, take up, take over; put up, put by, put out, put away, put on, put in*—the lists seem endless. For learners, the real difficulty lies in using such verbs productively, however, rather than understanding them, so it is fine to use them in explanations. A problem of understanding could arise, nevertheless, if several such variants were used in close proximity, without sufficient context, in the same computer application, in the same user interface. There are sometimes very commendable reasons for using phrasal verbs (they are very common in English, and can help to convey ideas that might seem daunting), but their environment must be studied closely to avoid introducing any possibility of confusion. A related point is that the "toggle" principle expressed in English through "on" and "off" (e.g., *switch on/switch off*), through "up" and "down" (e.g., *scroll up/scroll down*), and through "in" and "out" (e.g., *zoom in/zoom out*) cannot always be translated as a toggle—other languages use different verbs for each state—so this will sometimes have a bearing on interface design.

Confusion can also occur when it is difficult for users to tell whether the word they are looking at is a noun or a verb (e.g., *frame, block, chart, file, page, screen, release, index, search*). If a user chooses an option marked *index*, will an index appear, or will a document be indexed? *Search page* could start the process of searching a page (*search the page*), or it could take you to a special page for searching (*the search page*). An example involving *release* (*release processing*) was given in chapter 2.

Key Issues in Writing for Translation: Ambiguity, Culture

The concepts we have been considering so far in this chapter are all relevant to translation into another language and so to writing with a view to translation [see also Kirkman (1988)], but there are two more issues: ambiguity and culture. Ambiguity is all-pervasive in language. On the lexical level, in English, the most frequently used words are highly ambiguous, and this is particularly true of verbs; *have, take, move, go* are examples. Lytinen (1988) has explored the difference between words that are vague and those that are ambiguous, giving *went* as an example of a vague word (it has several related meanings, and needs refinement (e.g., *went to the store, went to California to start a new job*), and *draw* as an example of one that is "genuinely ambiguous" (the meanings are unrelated; e.g., *draw a picture, draw fans to a match*). Words that have the same form but are unrelated in meaning are known as *homonyms*. In the French language, some words are differentiated by gender, so they can be genuinely ambiguous when they stand completely on their own, such as on a screen button or menu (Box 19).

mémoire (f.)	memory
mémoire (m.)	dissertation, report
somme (f.)	sum, amount
somme (m.)	snooze
poste (f.)	postal services
poste (m.)	job, station, TV or radio set

Box 19. Some homonyms in French—
"genuinely ambiguous"

In the process of translation, dealing with ambiguity involves deciding whether the ambiguity is deliberate or accidental, and whether it should be reproduced or perhaps explained in the target language. In the computer environment, deliberate ambiguity seems most unlikely, but accidental ambiguity is almost guaranteed! When we were looking at grammar in chapter 2, we saw that the word "last" could be ambiguous in the expression "the last option" in English. Translating it into French, one would need to know which meaning was intended, since there are different words in French: *dernière* (last option in a list, only remaining option), or *précédente* (most recently used one). In a text, disambiguation normally takes place through contextual information as well as through reinforcement or redundancy. When one is dealing with individual words, those means are not available.

Apart from ambiguity, the second main area of difficulty in translation is centered on cultural references. A *cultural item* can be described as:

A word or phrase whose meaning in context may pose problems of comprehension to a non-native speaker for reasons other than its lexical unfamiliarity. . . . The identification of cultural items requires sufficient knowledge of source and target cultures to be aware of the opacity of certain references. The idea of opacity is of key importance: we must ask ourselves whether the reference is understood in both cultures, and if so, whether it is understood *in the same way*. (Back 1996, p. 2)

Some names of animals and plants have cultural connotations; for example, "poppy" denotes a flowering plant, but it connotes (is associated with) Armistice Day in Great Britain. Other cultural items refer to objects and institutions that are an integral part of the culture of a country, that do not exist elsewhere (e.g., Bonfire Night). In the context of computer applications, culture should be understood in the national sense as well as in the technological, social, and professional senses.

A different aspect of culture are writing styles that may not carry over into another language and culture. This is especially relevant to user guides and user documentation. A writing style that encapsulates a style of cultural interaction (e.g., informal and provocative or stilted and sticking to a formula) presents a translator with a very difficult problem, one that goes beyond the choice of words and phrases.

Filling Gaps in a Language

Nonequivalence at word level can involve culture-specific concepts, such as that of "privacy" in the British culture (Baker 1992), which carries the meaning of freedom from interference—we talk about "respecting someone's privacy." This is also represented by the expression "an Englishman's home is his castle." The concept goes some way toward explaining why there is so much *hedging* (leaving open a way of retreat) in British English: "I know you're really busy, so do tell me if you can't . . ."; "Would you mind awfully if . . . only I thought that maybe . . ."; "If you'd rather I didn't. . . ." Concepts similar to "privacy" in other languages, equivalent to "private life" or "solitude," do not convey the same cultural meaning.

Nonequivalence also occurs when a concept exists in another language, but there is no single word to express it. Waern (1989) mentions the problem of trying to translate the word *default* into Dutch, German, and Swedish and finding that "there was no equivalent single word in any of these languages. The closest we could come was a phrase which in English would have meant roughly 'that which happens unless you do something else'—obviously rather a clumsy expression" (p. 251).

It can be impossible to find an equivalent when there is no suitable word at the same level of abstraction; for instance the high-level word "facilities" has no equivalent in several languages. Very specific words denoting types of object known only in one setting can also cause problems. Translators sometimes use higher level (superordinate) words as part of their translation strategy. Parts of words, especially beginnings and endings (prefixes and suffixes) can be conveyors of meaning in one language (e.g., *trainer—trainee*), but not be easily transferable to another.

Sometimes the relationship between concepts is that of overlap: There is some common ground, but also there are differences. To give some examples from French and English, the word *document* is wider in scope of meaning in French than in English; in French, it can be used to refer to books, notes, papers, evidence, materials, and so on, as well as to documents. Conversely, the English word *report* corresponds to the French *rapport*, but also to *compte-rendu, reportage, communiqué, critique*. Similarity of form can be misleading and confusing. The word *directory*, as used in computing, would be *répertoire* or *dossier* in French, rather than *directoire*, which is a company's board of directors. The English words *education, training,* and *learning* do not have exact equivalents in French, and so forth.

Multiple Language Environments

The term "globalization" (or "internationalization") has recently begun to anchor itself in the vocabulary of user interface design. A very practical and richly illustrated book by Fernandes (1995) deals in a lively way with issues such as visual language and culture, symbols and taboos, rituals, heroes, national languages, and differences in the physical world: how objects with similar functions look in different countries and cultures. It provides a number of guidelines to follow during the phase of product design.

Nielsen (1993) also gives us much food for thought in this area, devoting a chapter of his book to "International User Interfaces." He states, "More than half of the world's software users will soon be using interfaces that were originally designed in a foreign country" (p. 237). He goes on to describe a fair range of problems, reminding us, for example, that icons and color connotations are not necessarily universal, and that metaphors can present a problem, since not all metaphors will be meaningful to all cultures. He makes the point that translators need to understand designers' language choices if they are to be able to do their job well: "If translators know why a certain word was chosen in an interface, they can better choose a translation that has the same connotations" (p. 243). Are reasons for choice systematically recorded by interface designers? This should certainly be considered as part of system documentation.

Unfortunately, principles of good design can sometimes be in apparent conflict with the practical demands of internationalization:

> There is solid evidence that icons should be paired with text labels to make learning easier (Mayhew 1992), but we decided to use only a graphic symbol because text labels would make internationalization more difficult. (Wilson et al. 1994, p. 412)

This appears to be a conscious decision, doubtless justified at the time, to bypass the potential difficulties of translation, knowing that learning is being compromised, that users will lose out. One wonders whether the perceived difficulties and various possible translation solutions were looked at in any detail, or whether there was no time, no resource, and perhaps no in-house expertise readily available for that. Had such an exercise been undertaken, it might have shown that the difficulties often stem from the way that language is handled in the interface: For example, text labels are more difficult to translate than text. Lessons could have been learned from that, which might have fed into the design of future applications.

Computer applications with an international dimension are also those that are likely to be used for communication between people from different language backgrounds, such as *electronic communication and conferencing* and collaborative work environments. They give rise to the formation of new vocabularies and abbreviations that reflect new types of interaction as much as tasks or tools (e.g., *f2f* for "face-to-face" meetings, as opposed to computer-mediated meetings, an abbreviation that requires a sophisticated knowledge of English to unpack). Packages for *computer-assisted language learning* are another special category of software where languages "rub shoulders" with each other and create potential problems in the interpretation of meanings in the user interface. Discussion of these different environments has to take account of the role of context in language understanding as well as the effect of the medium of communication and the types of interaction it supports. This is explored in the next two chapters.

SIX

The Effect of Context

- In what way does *formatting a table* resemble *passing a ball*?
- Is "Press X" a definition of X?
- Does it matter whether we know how to talk about maps?
- Does learning always affect one's language?
- When should users hide something that does not exist?

"Context" is a word that is used freely and has many meanings. This chapter describes some of the different immediate contexts that apply to language. It shows the links between social conventions and meanings and how meaning is inferred.

Visual and conceptual metaphors are investigated here, with emphasis on how we talk about metaphors. Context is then further explored in relation to professional preoccupations, situations, and tasks. This leads up to an important final section on verbal context, in which we look at how words form bonds with other words that surround them.

What Is Meant by "Context"?

The idea of context and its effect on meaning was briefly introduced in chapter 2, where the point was made that, out of context, a word may have a range of possible meanings, but that within a specific setting, one "actualized" meaning emerges. Put another way, context can help to resolve the ambiguity of word meaning. But it does not always resolve ambiguity. This is partly because there are typically a number of contexts to consider simultaneously. One perspective on this, which has been mentioned earlier, is to see context (in the sense of "reality") as a set of concentric circles, with personal context at the center, surrounded by social, cultural, and intercultural contexts. Our main concern in this chapter is what might be referred to as the *immediate context*, which can be said to fall into three categories: *situational, verbal,* and *visual.* Visual context is treated again in chapter 7. Sometimes, if aspects of the immediate context are ill-defined or missing, ambiguity can persist.

Halliday (1978) has written about the "context of situation" in these terms:

> Language comes to life only when functioning in some environment. We do not experience language in isolation—if we did we would not recognize it as language—but always in relation to a scenario, some background of persons and actions and events from which the things which are said derive their meaning. (p. 28)

The statement "if we did we would not recognize it as language" is intriguing, and the assertion may seem implausible unless we call to mind the distinction between form and meaning. A possible interpretation of this statement might then be that we would recognize the form of the language (e.g., letters next to one another, forming words) but that this language would be devoid of meaning. "Scenario" is just another term for situational context; its effect on meaning is indisputable. Langford (1994, p. 133) discusses the meaning of *passing a ball* in various games and makes the point that the different rules and practices of the games change the nature of *passing*—its purpose and its method of performance. Put another way, the meaning of *passing a ball* changes with each scenario. An analogy with actions in a user interface is easy to make: *formulating a query, formatting a table, copying files,* and so on are different with each system, application, or task scenario.

Verbal context, in the sense of text or speech surrounding a particular word, is another vitally important influence on meaning. For example, a word like *form* has a multitude of meanings. As a noun ("a form," "the form"), it can mean shape, method, grade, style, model, mold, level of fitness, etiquette, and so on. In a computer application, a short verbal context such as *select a form* goes some way toward eliminating possibilities within this group of meanings, but in this case, further information is needed to completely remove the ambiguity. It could come from a more elaborate verbal context; through a connection to the everyday or professional activity and specific task to which the word refers, or through visual means if possible (an image of a form). Box 20 shows a sample of words that have the potential to cause difficulties for users because of their wide range of meanings.

There are two distinct ways of viewing the importance of context. One of them is to see it as an *extra element in meaning,* the other is to consider it as being *crucial.* Lexicographers (dictionary compilers) and terminographers (compilers of specialized dictionaries) are constantly engaged in debate of the relative merits of definitions and contexts as purveyors of meaning. They

form	set	clear
entry	break	active
block	code	reference
case	note	record

Box 20. Sample of words with a
wide range of meanings

are still trying to decide whether meaning can be adequately represented without reference to context, and whether the right contextual information can ever replace definitions. We can say that X means different things depending on context and then set forth the various possibilities. But when faced with X in discourse—in a text or in speech—it becomes clear that its context can actually define its meaning. In that sense, *press X* defines X as being a button or key; *underline X* defines X as being a string of characters, and so forth. The two extremes of opinion can be expressed as follows:

- meaning *depends on* context
- meaning *is* context

Conventional and Inferential Meaning

We are now getting to the heart of the problem of meaning: Who or what defines meaning? Is it context, is it speakers of the language, is it lexicographers and terminologists? Word meaning is said to be "conventional," which is to say that as speakers of a language, we consent to meanings, we agree about meanings. Usage of a word by an individual person gradually becomes accepted usage through the social process of consent. Prototypes of meaning emerge (see chapter 3) in relation to shared assumptions about meanings. Evidence of usage is found in discourse and can support the claim that there is agreement about meaning:

Speakers define their membership of particular social groups by using forms which are peculiar to them, and in choosing a form which includes them as members of the group, they exclude others from it. (Brown et al. 1994, p. 4)

Is it ever necessary to spell out conventions by writing them down? One of the conventions used in this book is that words commonly used in user interfaces to applications (e.g., *file, open, form, option, copy*, etc.) appear in italics; italics are also used for emphasis. It is possible to gather that fact from simply reading the book, so what might be the advantage of drawing the reader's attention to it, such as in a list of conventions? Dictionaries record meanings (i.e., meaning conventions) for a variety of reasons: so that people can check their understanding of particular words or symbols, for example. What happens when conventions are not recorded in an explicit way? There is a risk of misunderstanding, but we might decide to accept that risk if there are tradeoffs.

The *file* menu that appears in the "menu bar" of many popular application programs has become conventional up to a point. It usually signals a grouping of actions to be done on files. It is typically a trigger for a hidden menu that pops up or is pulled down by the user. The contents of that menu will differ from one system or application to another, from one version of software to the next, and sometimes from one operation to the next. We have to ask ourselves whether users have been included in the social process of consent that has thus defined the meaning of *file*. The picture that emerges is that of a social process that excludes users, since they are not part of the community of people who design applications. At best, users are consulted explicitly about their preferences, but they do not normally participate initially in the implicit agreements that create word meanings in this domain.

The user does not know in advance exactly what to expect from the *file* menu, although some possibilities may suggest themselves from past experience, in the form of remembered options, past actions, or other connotations. These are part of the *inferences* that the user makes in the face of incomplete knowledge. Harley (1995) suggests that there are generally two basic types of inference: *logical* and *pragmatic*. If we apply the distinction to this example, a logical inference from the word *file* (interpreted as a verb) might be the expectation that one will be able to "file" documents in the general language meaning of the verb "to file": to put away in a consecutively ordered space for future reference. In some *file* menus, the only option that comes close to that meaning is *save*, while other options are distant from it (e.g., *delete, close*). In a word processing application program, the text that a user is typing might become either a "file" or a "document," depending on what the user happens to do with it. From the user's point of view, that is not logical. Dix et al. (1993) describe a problem caused by the *save* and *delete* options being adjacent in a menu—it is easy to choose the wrong one by mistake. These options are classified as file-level operations. The classification is logical from the system's point of view, but not the user's. If *file* stands for *file-level operations*, then we must ensure that this is made known to users.

Pragmatic inferences are of two types: "*bridging* (backward) inferences," which help to maintain coherence, and "*elaborative* (forward) inferences," which bring in knowledge of the world. "We comprehend on the basis that there is continuity in the material that we are processing, and that it is not just a jumble of disconnected ideas" (Harley 1995, p. 217). Just as that statement is applicable to texts and discourse in general, so it makes sense to ensure that a menu of options is coherent from the user's point of view—never a jumble of seemingly disconnected choices.

Talking About Metaphors

As we have seen in the section above, inferences are means of filling in missing knowledge. When we present users with *metaphors*, we are asking them
to make inferences. Metaphors are nonliteral interpretations of meaning. In a
discussion of the nature of "iconic signs" (images, diagrams, and metaphors)
Pelc (1986) defines metaphor as "a figure of speech based on comparison"
(p. 7), which accents important properties of the object it refers to. We can
say that in order to interpret a metaphor correctly, one has to recognize these
"important properties"; for example, if passion is represented by fire, one has
to know that it can be just as consuming, difficult to extinguish, and over-
whelming as fire. In the case of most words in the general language, a common understanding of important properties can be assumed. In specialized
areas, properties become a matter of special subject knowledge, and their
relative importance is something that only a specialist might be expected to
be able to judge. Besides, some computer users, but not necessarily all, will
be aware that metaphors have their limitations: Not all aspects of the meaning of one notion—however important they may be—can be transferred successfully to another notion.

As ever, context can be helpful in the interpretation of metaphor. In the
phrases "that's a rat" or "he's a rat," verbal context already provides a substantial clue as to which use is metaphorical. Situational and visual context
would further clarify the issue (cultural context might also be needed here).
A *visual metaphor* (e.g., a rat in a cartoon, depicting a person) requires visual
recognition as well as an interpretation of meaning. These are the challenges
we put before users when we face them with metaphors (e.g., *desktop, windows, noticeboard, whiteboard, form, ledger sheet, organizer, in-tray*). We
must therefore support them in the intended interpretation of meaning. Eco
(1986) tells us that only a mirror image is an "absolute" icon because "a mirror does not interpret an object" (p. 220). Other iconic signs do involve people
in an act of interpretation.

In the context of user interface design, Sorensen (1992) distinguishes between two levels in the use of metaphor: "the designer's latent perception of
what it means to use a computer system to carry out certain work tasks"
(p. 190) and the use of metaphors in the design of the actual screens of the
interface. The first level—the "latent" metaphor—is of special interest to
Sorenson, in that it has "a tendency to influence the language which develops in order to discuss and understand the potential and capacity" (p. 193) of
new technology. Sorensen discusses this with reference to computer conferencing systems and identifies four latent metaphors or perspectives: system,
dialog partner, tool, and medium. Each of these is said to produce a different
kind of language. For instance, the system perspective, where "humans are
perceived as machines" (p. 194), leads to command-based, technical language;
the dialog partner perspective generates linguistic responses that simulate

human interactions (e.g., "I don't understand") and is reflected in the way people communicate about the system (e.g., "and then it asks for my number").

When we consider the use of metaphors in the design of screens in the user interface, there is an important point to be made regarding the relationship between a visual or conceptual metaphor and language. Recognition of an object or action used in a metaphorical way (e.g., filing system, map, tree structure, game, schedule) does not mean that one is also familiar with the language used to talk about that object or action. For instance, I may be able to "read" and interpret a road map but may not be used to talking about such a map explicitly. In a computer environment, a road map metaphor could be useful, but if getting the most out of the road map required use of language, as opposed to spatial navigation, then its usefulness would depend on how the language aspect was handled in the interface. In a reasonably complex application, spatial navigation alone might not be enough to answer a user's questions:

- "How long will it take me to get from A to B in terms of completing all the tasks along the way?"
- "How important is this place on the map?"
- "Which place has the information I need?"

The user becomes engaged in a kind of game. How are the rules of the game to be explained to the user? Klein (1982) has remarked that people soon get confused when they try to explain a complex game because a game is not "prestructured by the temporal order of events" (p. 168). In other words, it is not in narrative form. Actual ordering is introduced by following the running of the game, which makes explanation easier.

In the map navigation example, there would be three options with regard to choice of language from a design point of view:

1. Use the specialized language of map navigation (but the map is only a visual metaphor here);
2. Use the language of computing (but can it be made to correspond to users' thinking?);
3. Start from the users' language by getting users to think aloud as they explore the spatial environment of a prototype map within a planned application. Then work out the links between the users' terms and possible computing terms through common underlying concepts. Subsequently incorporate users' language into support mechanisms (e.g., explanations, help facilities, tables of contents, indexes), based on a narrative structure if appropriate.

The need for a user to construct an object based on a metaphor raises the same issues. If we think of a table metaphor (derived from an arrangement of numbers or letters, typically a spreadsheet, not the article of furniture!), there are several levels:

- purely physical interaction—e.g., drawing lines, writing in the boxes formed
- verbal description using everyday words (thinking or thinking aloud) —e.g., "I'll put it on this line," "I'll group these figures together," "The total will go here";
- verbal interaction that typically requires a command of a specialized language—e.g., "select row," "delete cells," "left justify"

Designers often use metaphors among themselves at the stage when an application is being conceived and conceptualized. The metaphors used may be very colorful or grounded in everyday reality or make reference to other systems and applications. They can therefore seem inappropriate for explicit use in the language on the computer screen. Still, if a metaphor proves useful to designers, there is a chance it could be useful to users in understanding the system. One would need to proceed with great caution in this area, checking first that there is a shared understanding of the metaphor based on common culture or experience as appropriate. But there will be instances when the shared metaphor can be used in explanations addressed to the user, and the user will be able to learn by analogy. The structures and explicit relationships between entities that are key features of the design process are often obscured when the design is translated into a representation for users; for example, a hierarchical design structure becomes a series of screens or pages in the user's view. Users can then be heard reconstructing the structure as they talk about the application: "When you get to the next level . . . ," "How do I get back to the overview . . . ," and so forth. If we listen to this talk and capture it (e.g., by recording it), we can sometimes incorporate users' terms into the language of the interface or in explanations, correcting their misconceptions if necessary. This type of approach is used in foreign language teaching, where translation activities show up learners' misconceptions about correspondences between two languages. It also happens in more informal ways; for example, when a teacher walks around in a class, listening to groups of learners formulating sentences in their native language and then transfering them into the foreign language for a given task. Common mistakes are picked up by the teacher and explained and then used to plan further learning activities that incorporate words and expressions used by learners.

We must make the point very clearly now that there are two different language-related aspects to the interpretation of metaphor in user interface design. One aspect is enabling users to understand the nature of the metaphor and its limitations and to make positive use of the comparisons it allows (learning by analogy). Carroll, Mack, and Kellogg (1990) have provided a structured methodology for developing user interface metaphors that addresses the managing of "mismatches" in different ways, including on-line help that "can anticipate the consequences of user actions stemming from invalid mappings and guide users to alternative actions and to useful conclusions" (p. 81). Anderson et al. (1994) have given a useful technique for assessing the amount of "conceptual baggage" in any metaphor used within the context of a particular system, that is, features of the real world entity that do not apply to that system.

The second aspect, quite different from the first, has to do with giving users access to the language needed to make best use of an interface based on a particular metaphor. Support mechanisms, such as on-line help, can systematically provide the vocabulary and the phraseology for verbalizing or articulating the metaphor for productive use as well as for comprehension. It is also an opportunity to explain to users some of the language problems arising out of the use of *mixed metaphors*. Different metaphors can coexist better in the visual sphere, as graphic representations on the screen, than in the realm of language. To follow *a thread in a tree structure* sounds odd, but the visual representation can be unremarkable because we easily accept the figurative meanings of *tree* and *thread*—in an on-line course forum, for instance (Box 21).

Tools in a file, icons in windows and *items in a calendar* (as mentioned in chapter 1) can all sound rather dissonant when first encountered, depending on one's prior knowledge of the individual terms in a computer setting. Visual illustrations are vital in such cases to explain their meaning.

Metaphors are an important theme in relation to users' language and interface design; they are mentioned again when we explore "idioms" in relation to verbal context and in chapter 7, part of which deals with visual aspects of language and with the visualization expected of users by virtue of the electronic medium and the activity of interaction.

```
Introducing ourselves
    Course tutors
    Support staff
        Technical adviser
        Information officer
    Students
        Group A
        Group B
        Sorry I am late—problems connecting
            To help you catch up . . .
                Thanks for the help
                    Remember to join a group
                        Can't I work alone?
```

Box 21. Looking at a thread in a tree

Socioprofessional and Technological Contexts

The social and professional context in which we operate, circumscribed by subject area and function (e.g., education, business, law, medicine, administration, consultancy, training, facilitation, control, etc.) makes us choose words and structures appropriate to that context. It is one of the factors that determine the meanings we assign to words. Computer users in a business environment, for instance, have particular concerns related to business functions. These will include problem solving, decision making, scheduling and planning, information management, people management, financial management, quality control, and so on. Computer users in an educational setting might be concerned with learning and teaching effectiveness, achievement, assessment, access to materials and resources, and others. In medicine, the focus will perhaps be on diagnosis and treatment, clinical information about patients, laboratory results, and so forth (Alpay et al. 1995). Whatever the context, users are often looking for a "better way" of doing things, so that is also an important issue. Each of these can be overriding concerns, which is to say that they can color the way that users interpret language and conceive their own needs within a given application interface.

The influence of social and professional context—especially the feeling of "belonging" to a socioprofessional group—can be very strong. There can be a feeling of belonging to a *culture*, in the sense of a community of like-minded people, people with similar values and ways of thinking. As noted earlier, the people and ideas associated with information technology can be identified as a special kind of culture. From one perspective, this can be part of a technological world view, and, as such, it can be in conflict with the concerns of users who do not share that view.

Computer applications are intrinsically inseparable from technology because of their physical presence in a computer or network, though it is often possible to disguise and loosen the connection in various ways through the design of the interface. For some users, the expectation is that technology is incomprehensible, so there is an immediate barrier to be overcome. There may be an awareness of objects and processes, but not of their nature, since often there is much that is hidden from view. Users may have to guess at the likely outcomes of their actions and choices. *Clicking* with a mouse or selecting an item on the screen can be a risky business if users are unable to predict what will happen. Will there be a further selection to be made? Will a process begin? Can it be stopped? Will an explanation appear? This is quite an issue in the design of pages for the World Wide Web, because readers of Web pages need to know where they will end up and what software might be downloaded to their machine, if, as in Box 22, they do *click here*.

The technological context that is of most immediate relevance to a user's understanding is the particular application being used. In an environment that is not dedicated to just one application, users can experience difficulty in their

> For an example, click *here*
> Click *here* to see the movie
> More information available *here*

Box 22. What will happen next?

orientation within the environment, which affects their understanding. Writing about his experience with students at Hull University, Reese (1996) remarks that "Many students are rather vague as to what they are using: a typical enquiry starts with, 'I was typing into Windows when . . .'" (p. 1).

He goes on to say that the problems faced by students in an application like Microsoft Word stem from the particular features of the software. The action of "deleting" is one example of this: Highlighting a complete text and pressing the ENTER key (which may be done accidentally) *deletes* the text in the sense that the user now sees a blank screen; in fact, the text has been copied to a clipboard and can be restored, but not all users know this. The consequences of a deleting action vary depending on what is being deleted. A footnote is not removed just by deleting the footnote text (its "marker" in the document must be deleted); a user can thus be under the illusion of having completed an action, when in fact there is something else that must be done. Nielsen (1993, p. 128) refers to a similar problem with a *delete file* command that does not completely remove the contents of the file, only makes the storage space occupied by the file available for use by other files at a later date. Users who have not been made aware of this will not realize that their file contents may still be accessed—by intruders, for instance. Representing the command by a paper shredder icon can make matters worse, as the act of shredding is wrongly connoted.

So, in a more general sense, an understanding of how computers work and what thay are capable of doing is now needed by users if they are to make best use of an application. Something as basic as the realization that computers habitually keep a record of recent operations can make a difference to the way a user will perceive an *undo* command, for instance: Can you *undo* just one operation or a whole sequence? If there is no recognizable *undo* option, is the action irreversible?

Situational and Task Factors in Language

When we consider a user's immediate concerns, these are linked to the situation the user is currently in and the task to be accomplished. Place and time constraints become relevant, such as working with others or alone, communicating through an intermediary or directly, in difficult or easy conditions, working to a deadline or at leisure. A "task" as we understand it here might be about getting information, distributing messages, organizing documents, combining different media, making calculations, simulating a problem, and so on. These are quite specific actions or activities. Accomplishing them requires skill, experience, and knowledge. It is not our intention here to enter into the details of these tasks but rather to show that situational and task factors have an impact on how language might be used in the application interface. Phillips et al. (1990) describe a method that defines operational requirements in terms of user tasks and transforms these tasks into dialog design elements. The approach we take is directed at the language necessary to describe and to perform various tasks. Diaper (1989) makes the point that verbal data from users are needed for task analysis and can be obtained through various means, such as interviews, think-aloud protocols, and post-task walkthroughs. We can hypothesize that the language will reflect some of the formal elements of task analysis, such as descriptions of goals, overall and subordinate operations, and planned sequence. One would also expect elements that focus on responsibility for actions, on authority, and on control.

In this section we first consider *learning, exploring*, and *searching*, and then *decision-making*. We will take learning to be more purposeful than exploring, normally directed by a teacher or an external goal. For our purposes here, to explore is to extend the boundaries of one's knowledge as an end in itself or in a self-directed way. Exploration may happen even if it is not anticipated. Jones et al. (1995), describing the use of computer-based instructional materials on a U.K. Open University course, make the following remark:

> Nearly half of the students experimented and explored and only read the manual as a last resort. Such an approach can create a tension between students' working styles and the assumptions of the instructional materials. It was argued that this active approach to learning suggests that unexpected use of instructional material is normal or even desirable: we need to facilitate exploration and experiment whilst protecting students from the worst pitfalls of their own discoveries. (p. 8)

The user interface to applications designed for any of these ends (learning, exploration, or searching) is a gateway to intellectual *skills* as well as to *content*. The skills and abilities that may need to be used include comparison, analysis, evaluation, synthesis, interpretation, application, and questioning. When we are thinking about how the user will gain access to content, it is important to remember that the content has a number of potential knowledge structures; for instance, that it can be comparative, and analytical in nature, and that elements of content can be brought together for comparison, can form a sequence in response to a question, and so forth. The basic structure of knowledge is said to have three components: categories, rules for category membership (distinctive features), and category interrelations. The distinctive features and the links between categories of knowledge should be accessible to users.

It is not easy to reconcile a user's potentially wavering or fuzzy language, which reflects the process of grappling with incomplete knowledge, with the definitive, self-assured nature of statements in a help facility or user manual. In most areas, except for those that are focused on the development of physical skills, the process of learning involves changes in one's language that are essential rather than incidental to the process. This means that to create a context conducive to intellectual and social learning is also to cater to the language development that will be taking place. It also means acknowledging that there is an *affective* side to learning, "concerned with feelings, values, and commitments" (Rowntree 1981, p. 188). In terms of user interface design, the implications are that users need to be helped to develop their language together with their confidence and attitudes appropriate to their subject field.

A fundamental feature of learning is the need to restudy material previously visited, not just for reinforcement and practice, but also in order to exercise some of the skills we have mentioned: comparison, evaluation, synthesis, interpretation, and so forth. The language that is potentially associated with these contexts is:

- the language of *questions* (How does X relate to Y? Is X better than Y? How important is X? What are the main features of X? Does X have this meaning? Is there more to X than this? What happens if . . . ? What is someone else's view on X? How do I do X? How have others done X?)
- the more abstract language of the *intellectual operations* implicated in those questions (compare, assess usefulness or importance, extract key elements, interpret meaning, enquire about boundaries, form opinion, obtain guidance)
- the language of *knowledge tracking* (I know this but not that; I know this well; I learned this but don't know it; I can't see the bigger picture)
- the language of *learning method* (need to gather facts, to remember, to practice, to note, to list, to reflect, to see an illustration)
- the language of *learning objectives and outcomes* (achievement, success or failure, passing a test, completing learning modules, gaining an understanding, becoming competent, being able to solve a problem)

Kumaravadivelu (1991, 1993), writing about language learning tasks in a classroom setting, emphasizes the potential mismatch between teacher intention and learner interpretation. To help the teacher analyze tasks, potential sources of mismatch are given. The list includes communicative skills and strategies, linguistic repertoire required to problem solve, prior knowledge of the target culture norms, attitudes, and expectations. There are also sources of mismatch in the cognitive, strategic, tactical, evaluative, pedagogic (objectives), and instructional (giving directions) aspects of teacher-learner interaction. All these are relevant categories for thinking about tasks in computer-assisted learning.

The naming of tasks is worth thinking about in relation to their perception by users. Is there a difference between an *ad hoc search* and a *document search* purely from the point of view of how they have been named? One name refers to type or frequency of search, while the other emphasizes place or scope. If the search facility in question could be given either name, then we must ask: Which aspect is more important to users?

Learning, exploring, and searching overlap with decision making, especially since much of learning involves acquiring the skills implied in decision making and learning through them. A study carried out by Hubona and Blanton (1996) contrasted perceived "usefulness" and "ease of use" of interface features in decision making tasks. It showed that "perceived ease of use contributes significantly to enhanced levels of user confidence in decision quality. Moreover, user interfaces perceived as easy to use are associated with faster and more accurate decisions" (p. 93). Conversely, interfaces perceived as more useful, rather than easy to use, resulted in users taking longer to make decisions that were no more accurate, and user confidence in decision quality was not promoted. Given that easy communication is one of the factors in ease of use of an interface, these results are well worth noting.

The traditional grammar concept of modality (first mentioned in chapter 2) is important in the sphere of decision-making: Can I do this? should I? must I? are some of the question forms that accompany decision-related thinking. In other words, this thinking is expressed through modal verbs or "auxiliaries": *can, could, would, should, ought, might, may, have to, had to, must.* Box 23 shows some questions that represent this sphere [the subject area is computer security; for full details, see Kukulska-Hulme (1993)].

- How often *should* I change my password?
- *Should* I be using data encryption for communications traffic?
- How easy *would* it be for someone to hack into the system?
- *Must* I have access control on my PC?
- How often *must* passwords be changed?
- *Can* I have a document folder that only I can access?
- *Can* the system help me to identify vulnerable areas?
- Do I *have to* sign off every time I leave my computer?

Box 23. Decision-making: use of modal verbs

Surrounding Words: Verbal Context

At the start of this chapter some remarks were made about the expression *select a form*, which provides a very brief verbal context for the word *form*. Sinclair (1991) prefers the term *co-text*: "The co-text of a selected word or phrase consists of the other words on either side of it" (p. 172). The idea of verbal context also takes us back to what was said earlier about patterns in language in relation to grammar. *Select a form* is a pattern made up of two grammatical parts of speech—a verb and a noun; we can also describe it as a combination of a *base term* (*select*) with one of its *collocates* (*a form*). The base term *select* has many other collocates in the language of computing (e.g., *select an option, select a command, select text, select a frame*) and fewer in the general language.

Collocations (regularly occurring combinations of words) are classified according to the strength of the relationship between the words involved. A *frozen collocation* or *fixed phrase* is a combination in which none of the components can be moved, replaced, or left out, and no new element can be added without changing the meaning (e.g., *bird of paradise, as a matter of fact*). In the language of computing, "compound terms" are common examples of frozen collocations, such as *custom dictionary* and *document template*, but it is wise to consider these as being frozen in the context of one particular system. In a wider context, the same collocations can be deemed to be *restricted* rather than frozen (for instance, there is a wider, but not infinite, range of dictionary types used in computing), whereas in the general language, they can be much more *free*. Pavel (1994) uses the above classification in her *Guide to Phraseology Research in Languages for Special Purposes*.

Collocations overlap with *idioms*. Sinclair (1991) explains that the difference between collocations and idioms is not obvious:

> They both involve the selection of two or more words. At present, the line between them is not clear. In principle, we call co-occurrences idioms if we interpret the co-occurrence as giving a single unit of meaning. If we interpret the occurrence as the selection of two related words, each of which keeps some meaning of its own, we call it a collocation. (p. 172)

Wide of the mark would typically be considered an idiom, because the words form a single unit of meaning. Many authors associate idioms with figurative, nonliteral meaning. Figurative expressions are often picturesque in character; *flog a dead horse, like a lead balloon, back to the drawing board, keep one jump ahead, in the red* [see Urdang and LaRoche (1980) for more examples]. There is further overlap here with so-called *catch phrases*—usually self-contained colloquial expressions with humorous or ironic overtones, such as *Good question! Not if I can help it; That's your best bet; Now he tells me! Back to square one; I believe you—thousands wouldn't* (Partridge 1977).

"Idioms suffer terrible indignities within linguistics, philosophy, and psychology. Compared to metaphors, which are thought to be 'alive' and creative, idioms traditionally have been viewed as dead metaphors or expressions that were once metaphorical, but that have lost their metaphoricity over time" (Gibbs 1993, p. 57). Gibbs argues that idioms are very much alive: Speakers make sense of idioms because of the metaphorical knowledge that motivates these phrases' figurative meanings. Metaphorical knowledge consists of mental images, so, for example, phrases like *flip your lid*, *blow your stack*, and *lose your cool* are motivated by the metaphor "anger is heated fluid in a container." We can apply this argument to the domain of computing phraseology, where mental images play an important role. To understand *collapse an outline* and *expand an outline* in a document creation facility, one needs to be able to visualize the outline as a flexible entity, capable of being expanded and collapsed.

Collocations are an extremely important aspect of a language from the point of view of a language learner: a computer user, in our perspective. They are undoubtedly a key to finding out what might constitute "sufficient context" for understanding when the question arises in interface design. Let us take an actual example to illustrate the point. An action that is easily conceptualized in its traditional form can become very complex in a computer setting, requiring mastery of a number of terms and expressions. Page numbering by hand compared with page numbering in a word processing system is a case in point. Reese (1996) writes that students using Microsoft Word "come to the Helpdesk when they are unable to position, or delete, or print page numbers. They are confused by the sophisticated terminology and control for headers and footers" (p. 11). When we examine the terminology, it turns out that to understand *page numbering*, users should also understand *headers*, *footers, alignment, number format, frame, insertion point*, and *hiding*. These terms appear in on-line help and can be thought of as *co-occurrences* of the term *page numbering*, terms to be found in close proximity to the main term in text (strictly speaking, words co-occur on a regular basis, in texts of the same type and within a specified short distance of one another). In the on-line help, *page numbering* appears to require several actions, some of which are obligatory and some optional (e.g., *creating a footer, specifying page number alignment, positioning the insertion point*, and *hiding the page number on the first page*). There is a quick way of adding page numbers, using default settings, but the wide range of terms used in the explanations (which may be consulted first) has made many a timid user resort to page numbering by hand!

SEVEN

The Effect of Medium and Interaction

- Why are electronic texts suspect?
- Can you tear out a page on a screen?
- How does chopping up sentences make them coherent?
- When do actions speak louder than words?
- How can we use questions to map out knowledge needs?

We begin this chapter by looking at what is to be gained from understanding the relationship between *written* and *spoken* language. The consequences of putting words on the *screen* are explored, in terms of changes in the meaning of terms, pronunciation, and the effect of spatial proximity on meanings.

We then move on to consider aspects of *verbal interaction*, such as politeness and fluency, and conclude with an overview of users' knowledge needs identified by analyzing their language.

Relationship Between Speech and Writing

Written texts all have to be related somehow, directly or indirectly, to the world of sound, the natural habitat of language, to yield their meanings. (Ong 1982, p. 8)

The world of sound as "the natural habitat of language." Historically, and in an individual's development, speech comes before writing. For a small child, language is all speech. This is obviously not so for older children and adults, and for some, language is nearly all reading and writing. Still, for most people, language is strongly associated with sound, in a concrete way through hearing and producing language as well as through mental association. In a situation where computers are used, spoken and written language are both present in some way (not necessarily at the same time), not least of all because it is most unusual for someone to use an application without ever speaking about its use!

In general, indirect reference from written language to sound through a reader's prior experience of spoken language or through a special notation is acceptable in many different circumstances, such as in books and newspapers. The question is, What, if anything, do we lose when real sound is missing? Physical demands on the reader (user) are now focused on visual processing. *Verification* of meaning, in terms of its expressive dimension and also being able to gauge whether a message is complete, which normally happens through listening to the melody of a phrase or sentence, now depends on *punctuation*. The problem with punctuation is that generally speaking it is not considered very important by people who are not language specialists or enthusiasts. Consequently it may be overlooked, wrongly interpreted, or misused, so in effect it cannot be said to replace intonation. However, users who do habitually pay attention to conventional punctuation symbols will definitely want those visual clues as part of the user interface and may also want their own use of punctuation to be correctly interpreted in interaction. Their concern with punctuation may come from their educational background, the type of work they do, or the intrinsic importance of language in a given application (e.g., support for language learning, writing and editing, literary studies, etc.).

A particular issue connected to spoken and written language, and relevant to HCI design, presents itself in relation to so-called "deictic verbs of motion," such as *come*, *go*, *bring*, and *take*. Tanz (1980) describes *deixis* as follows:

> When language is spoken, it occurs in a specific location, at a specific time, is produced by a specific person and is (usually) addressed to some specific other person or persons. Only written language can ever be free of this kind of anchoring in the extra-linguistic situation. A sentence on a slip of paper can move through space and time, "speaker"-less, and addressee-less. All natural, spoken languages have devices that link the utterance with its spatio-temporal and personal context. This linkage is called "deixis." (p. 1)

Does the written language in a user interface "move through space and time," without speaker or addressee? Some would argue that written language is never actually like that. Or is it language that happens for the user, at a specific location and time? An interface designer should form a view on this matter. The fact is that written language on the screen, being interactive in nature, is unlike most other types of writing.

There are significant benefits to be gained from seeing written language through the prism of the spoken. When it comes to making use of actual speech in computer systems, there are many problems, of course. Misconstructions due to mishearing or difficulty in recognition are possible when sound is involved. For nonnative speakers, aural comprehension is the most difficult part of dealing with a foreign language. Besides, the speech signal is normally only available for a short time; it is ephemeral. Access to repetition of part of a message can be difficult. These are some important practical issues to consider when making user-centered decisions about media.

As pointed out by Halliday (1978), written language has a higher *lexical density* than speech, lexical density being the proportion of so-called lexical items (or content words) to words as a whole (content and function words). As defined by Spears (1991), *content words*—typicallly nouns, verbs, adjectives, and adverbs—are vocabulary words, the ones that convey lexical meaning, whereas *function words* have a grammatical meaning and include prepositions (e.g., *about, at, for, from, in, with*), negative particles (*not, no*), and conjunctions (*if, although, or, unless*).

However, Halliday goes on to say that pragmatic language, the "language of action," has the lowest lexical density of all. This is interesting, since in a user interface, what one normally sees are predominantly content words, but the function of the language is centered on action, a contradiction that surely is the source of many communication problems in that environment. Spears' dictionary contains a function word index that could be useful to anyone wanting to examine the use of these words in interfaces to systems that are being developed.

Written language is associated with a certain formality that can set up psychological barriers and be at odds with effective communication. At the opposite end of the scale, ostentatious informality, which is certainly possible in writing, can also have a negative effect on some people. Self-teaching materials are interactive in nature and therefore tend to cross the boundary between spoken and written language. Rowntree (1981) has written that well-designed self-instruction materials must carry out all of the functions that a teacher would carry out in the conventional situation: motivating, guiding, explaining, provoking, reminding, asking questions, appraising, and so on.

Language used in a computer-mediated communication environment (e.g., text-based computer conferencing) also shares some of the features of speech and of writing. More than that, as a vehicle for group communication, "computer conferencing possesses unique features which make it qualitatively different from either spoken or written communication" (Kaye 1992, p. 17); it allows reflective and thoughtful analysis, while at the same time increasing opportunities for interaction and participation. The language used in interfaces to conferencing and discussion software often reflects these disparate ends; there may be words relating to reflective pieces of writing, such as *con-*

tribution and *paper*, and also words suggesting quick exchanges (e.g., *message*, *note*, *comment*), mixed up in the same environment. The written record of on-line interactions has been described as "preserved conversation" (Mason 1992, p. 4), a combination of preserved documents and conversational interactions.

The Screen Environment for Words

The perceived validity of any message depends on the medium. In former times, the written word was held in high esteem, but the electronic word is suspect. What exactly is its source if not properly identifiable? Has the source been evaluated? Has the text been corrupted in transit? Has it been copied without acknowledgement (i.e., plagiarized)? On-screen help text and printed documentation are not normally attributed to an expert's name (or at least the name is not immediately visible); they may well be less credible for that.

The main strengths of the screen environment for words are, first, its unfinished quality—the user can sometimes be given the opportunity to change words or annotate—and its potential to adapt to users' changing needs over time. The ability to browse, potentially a strength, is often deceptive, promising more than it delivers, because so much is obscured from the user's view and discernment. An important weakness is that screen text is more difficult to read than typewritten text (Moskel et al. 1984). The constraints of space on the screen are also responsible for the compressed language that is often favored; for example, a message that simply says: *invalid option.*

The screen environment borrows metaphors from paper media (*forms, books, notebooks, sticky labels,* etc.) and in doing so calls their names into question. What is a notebook, for instance, once it is on the computer screen? Assumptions about the way it looks and how it may be used are challenged. Can you tear out pages, for instance? The problem is that the label may well stay the same (*notepad, logbook, handbook, calendar, directory, out-tray,* etc.), whereas the meaning behind it changes in the minds of its creators. That change or elaboration of meaning should be communicated to prospective users, but this does not always happen.

Visual Aspects of Language

Anyone interested in the visual aspects of texts would do well to read Tonfoni (1994), which casts the writer in the role of painter, drawer, and architect, and explores the physical shape of texts in space. In this section we look at some visual aspects of words, including their spelling, and also at the effect of spatial relationships between words on the screen on the interpretation of their meaning.

If you were to see the word "yes" spelled "ye-e-es," what tone would it have for you—emphasis or hesitation? Variations in letter size, shape, and spacing provide a wide range of possible effects in written language. This can be a great advantage in communication, but it depends on a shared understanding of the meanings and cultural connotations of particular styles and conventions. Italics, underlining, and capital letters, for instance, all vary in usage depending on context. Not all languages allow use of italics or have the equivalent of capital letters, which means that semiconventional uses of these typographical features may be lost on users of English language software who are nonnative speakers.

An important visual aspect of the English language is the irregularity of English spelling: *key* and *quay* are prime examples of different spellings for words that sound the same. *Move, dove,* and *cove* further illustrate the indirect relationship between pronunciation and spelling. At other times, it is subtle differences in pronunciation that cause problems. For instance, many native speakers write *of* where *off* is needed (e.g., "take the top of the container"), and the mistake is not picked up by spelling checkers. People reading a phrase containing the incorrect word will disregard the mistake if the intended meaning is obvious. Nonnative speakers are more likely to be perplexed by the effect on meaning if they are unaware that this is a common spelling mistake. They are also liable to mispronounce a difficult or unusual word (e.g., *redo, undo, goto*) and so may well be unable to make the connection between form and meaning or end up making an incorrect connection (e.g., *debt* can become *debit* if all the letters are sounded!). *Forward* and *foreword* are a pair of words that are often confused because they sound the same.

Punctuation helps readers to determine how each word is to be pronounced. It can make comprehension easier, together with other visual means such as layout. Dividing up a sentence visually into phrases can be helpful in conveying meaning. Placing it in a delimited space can make it more visually pleasing and easier to read. Compare this sentence with the same one in the previous paragraph:

> Nonnative speakers
> are more likely to be perplexed
> by the effect on meaning
> if they are unaware
> that this is a common spelling mistake.

Sentences and texts produce in readers an expectation of continuity and coherence, which is important in the process of comprehension. In contrast to this, single words in menus, toolbars, and indexes on the screen create a visual context and expectation that, because they are close together physically, they are also related semantically. A series of options that includes "help," for instance, can build up the expectation that the "help" option is directly related to the other ones and that it helps the user to understand them:

File Edit Copy Text References Map Utilities Help

In this example, if users want to know what the *Copy* option is for, can they go to *Help* to find out, or must they choose *Copy* and see what happens (hopefully nothing untoward)? In this instance, *Help* should explain the other options as well as giving other information or advice that might be needed in the application.

Another type of problem can occur when a set of options includes one that is called *Options* or when a menu invites users to *Display a menu*, as in the example in Box 24. This shows the toolbar of an emulation window across the top and below it is part of the IBM AS/400 Main Menu. What meaning does *Options* have when a user is already looking at what appear to be options? What does *Display a menu* mean when one is looking at a menu?

Conversation and Interaction

Much has been written about the various types of verbal exchange that lie at the heart of language-based communication. Most of this comes under the designations of "conversation analysis" and "dialog design." Brief, lucid introductions to the structure of conversation are given in Harley (1995, p. 239) and in Graddol, Cheshire, and Swann (1994, p. 162). Fromkin and

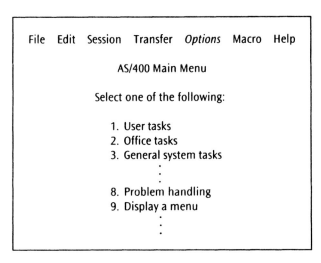

Box 24. IBM AS/400: options within options, a menu within a menu (emphasis added)

Rodman (1993) explain the "maxims of conversation" (cooperation, relevance); they also give a very simple account of "speech acts," as introduced
by Searle (1970), which are acts performed through language and typified by
verbs such as *promise, warn,* and *nominate* [actually, in their view, "every
utterance is some kind of speech act" (p. 160)]. Specifically in relation to HCI,
Hindus (1991) has applied conversational models to interactive system design. Turn-taking in conversation and the theory of speech acts are very well
covered in a substantial chapter on "CSCW Issues and Theory" in Dix et al.
(1993). While emphasizing that these topics are all very important, we will
not go over the exact ground here.

"Verbal interaction is perhaps the most important variety of language use"
(Langford 1994, p. 185). Langford explains how one can set about the investigation and analysis of everyday talk, and he makes a helpful distinction
between "speech activities" and "speech events." *Speech activities* are verbal interactions taking place during other activities such as eating a meal or
learning to drive, and *speech events* are episodes that are all about talk, such
that they "begin and end with the talk that they involve" (p. 157). Examples
of speech events are chats, conversations, discussions, and talks. In an office
environment, a conversation may be held through an exchange of written notes
between colleagues if they do not have time to talk properly but only pick up
messages between meetings, and it might imitate a speech activity or event.
Human-computer interaction can be similar in character, although the potential for informality, "shorthand," and humor cannot be released to the same
extent nor in the same way.

In effect, verbal interaction is severely constrained in its simulated forms in
a computer setting. In Wiklund (1994), there is a drawing that carries the message: "Making technology as friendly as the family pet." This is a most appealing goal, even if it is perhaps slightly tongue-in-cheek. At the same time, however, it is worth pointing out that it highlights a basic problem. We may have a
friendly relationship with our pet, we can talk to the pet, but—and here is the
difference—we cannot claim to understand fully what the pet is "saying." An
interactive and intuitive relationship, certainly, but ultimately limited.

In human interactions, there is a moral obligation and social convention that
dictate that one normally gives a constructive answer in response to a colleague's
question or problem, or at least indicates where to look or whom to ask next. "I
don't know" on its own can sound brutish. The moral obligation is lacking in
computer systems, and the social convention is often neglected. Everyday tactics that make conversations polite, such as greetings, expressions of thanks,
apologies, and congratulations, translate with difficulty into the language of
human-computer interaction. *Politeness* may need to be expressed through
actions rather than words, through attentiveness to a user's needs, much as one
would behave when dealing with a visitor from a foreign country whose language one did not know well or at all. If some language communication were
possible in that situation, one might, for instance, try to find out beforehand

what would be offensive or perplexing to that person and make sure those words and gestures were never used. Users are sometimes artificially forced into polite behavior when they have no other option but to respond *OK* to an error message rather than "Why not?" or "What do I do now?"

Something that all speakers come to expect is that a normal conversation will not be totally fluent: *hesitation, pauses, false starts,* and *repetitions* will naturally occur. Courtesy dictates that we do not draw attention to those "errors," so we either do not react to them, or if we do, it is in an encouraging and helpful way. By contrast, in computer applications, some sort of response is normally given to all input, however tentative it may be, and this response can appear stark and feel unwelcome. Words in every response must be chosen so that they are appropriate to potentially nonfluent input. What really matters is that it should be easy for users to backtrack: the physical equivalent of "I didn't mean that" or even "I didn't say that."

Elements of Questions: Articulation of Needs

Users' questions, whether formulated explicitly or not, are an essential starting point in thinking about how an application might be designed to answer them. One of the most exciting aspects of questions is that it is possible to identify categories of users' knowledge needs by examining the language of questions. Table 3 shows an example of a knowledge-need overview produced as a result of an analysis of users' questions in the field of computer security.

Table 3. Knowledge need overview

Actions	Events
Knowing *What* to do:	*What* happens:
What do I do?	What happens?
Knowing *When* to do something:	*When* something happens:
When do I do this?	When does this happen?
Knowing *How* to do something:	*How* something happens:
How do I do this?	How does this happen?
Knowing *Where* to do something:	*Where* something happens:
Where do I do this?	Where does this happen?
Knowing *Why* to do something:	*Why* something happens:
Why do I do this?	Why does this happen?
Knowing *Who* does something:	*Who/what* is affected:
Who does this?	Who does this happen to?
Knowing *Whether* one does something:	*Whether* something happens:
Do I do this?	Does this happen?
Knowing *Whether* one *Can* do something:	*Whether* something *Can* happen:
Can I do this?	Can this happen?
Knowing *Whether* one *Should* do something:	*Whether* something *Should* happen:
Should I do this?	Should this happen?

Adapted from Kukulska-Hulme (1993).

What is most striking about this information is that, at least in that particular field, users can be seen to have areas of concern that are much richer in scope than what is typically admissible in applications—"How do I do this?" is only one type of question, even if it is a frequent one.

The point of this is not the processing of natural language queries to supply users with answers, however. It is to see if the identification of users' prime concerns—in this instance, dealing with timing, manner, location, cause, agent, possibility, advisability, and so on—can become the basis for the design of better user interfaces, retrieval mechanisms, and help facilities. It turns out that it is possible to take account of such findings. One way of doing this is to make use of the terms that express such concerns; for instance, "timing" is represented by words like *frequent*, *often*, and *regular*. This approach is further developed in chapter 9, which has a practical orientation and focuses on specific purposes and functions of language in the user interface.

III

LANGUAGES FOR SPECIAL PURPOSES AND FUNCTIONS

EIGHT

Labeling and Abbreviation

Labels, Terms, and Systems of Concepts

> Oral folk have no sense of a name as a tag, for they have no idea of a name as something that can be seen. Written or printed representations of words can be labels; real, spoken words cannot be. (Ong 1982, p. 33)

So many user interfaces have the appearance of a collection of labels, stuck onto invisible boxes whose contents remain a mystery to users until they have made the effort of opening up each box in turn and sifting through its contents. In order to explore what might be called "the language of labeling," we must first make some observations about the relationship between terms and concepts. *Terms* are words with special subject meanings; a term may consist of one or more "units" (e.g., *user interface*). As has been pointed out by Sager (1990), *concepts* are notoriously difficult to define; it is, however, possible to group them into four basic types:

- *class concepts* or entities, generally corresponding to nouns
- *property concepts* or qualities, for the most part corresponding to adjectives
- *relation concepts* realized though various parts of speech, such as prepositions
- *function concepts* or activities, corresponding to nouns and verbs

Looking at the relationship between terms and concepts will help us to think about whether terms can be used to label various types of knowledge and also whether they can properly represent users' knowledge needs. The present book is structured around linguistic "concepts" in the broad sense, whereas in this chapter, when we refer to concepts, it is in the narrower terminological sense indicated above.

"We can use any names we wish as labels for concepts so long as we use them consistently. The only other criterion is convenience" (Hudson 1995, p. 4). In special subject areas, these same criteria apply, except that communication of specialized knowledge obliges us to take account of how concepts have been labeled by others and how the concepts we are handling fit into a wider scheme.

We can draw up systems of concepts and try to specify relationships between them, uncovering along the way the knowledge structures that bind them together. However, we cannot do the same with terms. Terms are existential in nature, that is to say, they signal the existence of an entity, a relationship, an activity, or a quality. Considered outside of verbal context, terms can express neither facts not rules, and they can say nothing about the manipulation of knowledge. Furthermore, many concepts, particularly of the relational and functional types, are designated by words of general, not special, reference. For example, *of*, *to*, *in*, and *go* are words that are not normally regarded as terms.

In a situation where a user needs to obtain information from a computer system, how can a term represent a specific knowledge need, other than one that seeks only to discover the meaning of a term or to confirm the existence of a term or concept? The many different types and aspects of knowledge—procedural, functional, relational, control knowledge, and so on—are not well served by terms as symbols of knowledge in the context of satisfying users' needs. The language of labeling, which insists on discrete labels for knowledge representation appears to disregard their role in discourse, so in principle it is a poor vehicle for communication. Nonetheless, we can still look to see whether better use of labels and an extension of the language of labeling can make a difference to the quality of human-computer communication.

New Names for Old Concepts, Old Names for New

The question of appropriate use of labels brings us back to our earlier discussions revolving around language change. What do users understand by *Contents* as a facility within an application? "Tables of Contents" have been around for a long time, but in a computer setting they acquire new characteristics and new behavior. The label itself might change from being a heading for a list of contents to being a command, a request to see the contents. In addition to that, in a Windows environment, the contents of a window are the text and graphics in it, nothing to do with a table of contents. Similarly, the contents of a table are not necessarily topics! *Print Contents* becomes highly ambiguous in such an environment. Its correct interpretation may depend on noting the capital letter in Contents.

The label *Topics* is also used to indicate a "Table of Contents," in which case a new name has been given to an old concept, and the two names compete with each other as synonyms. The inevitable broadening and change of meanings creates an uncertain atmosphere for users. Examples of rapid change are not difficult to find. *Navigation* is a popular label in applications based on hypertext structures. In one such system designed for educational ends, *Navigation* was found to include information and advice intended to help students organize the time devoted to their studies. A time element can be included in the concept of navigation, but it is not one that immediately springs to mind, so the infomation behind the label is concealed by it.

Conference is a term whose definition can no longer assume a physical location. It may still be a meeting for consultation or discussion, but it may be held electronically and its assumed formal nature may not apply. So, for example, a Web site on the Internet that refers to a conference may need to be more specific about the type of conference that is envisaged (e.g., *on-line conference, electronic conference, annual conference*) if misunderstandings are to be avoided.

"Parts of Speech" in Labels

We have noted as we have gone along that the understanding of meaning depends to some extent on the "correct" pronunciation of words. We have also seen that it is difficult to conceive of a standard language. Standardization is an even less attainable goal with respect to pronunciation. Out of context, the word *progress* can be a noun or a verb; it depends on pronunciation, but regional accents can obscure this basis for distinction. Nonnative speakers can have real difficulties in noting differences in meaning that are dependent on pronunciation.

The adjectives *previous* and *next* are incomplete when they stand on their own and ambiguous when there is more than one object to which they may refer in a given application (e.g., *previous page, previous module, previous message, previous screen*). *Special* is another adjective often found on its own on toolbars and buttons. As already observed in chapter 2 a set of options that mixes different parts of speech is not helpful, but that principle on its own would not prevent a set of options that consisted of *next, previous,* and *special* only (all adjectives), so both considerations are important: same parts of speech in a set of options and complete phrases.

Uses and Values of Capital Letters

Design conventions that stipulate the use of capital letters at the beginning of words to indicate a special meaning (e.g., the name of a button: *Change Icon* versus *Change icon*) are not necessarily noticed and interpreted correctly by users. They may also be obscured by *competing conventions*, such as the use of capitals at the start of option names (e.g., *Index File* can mean something different than *index File*), or capital letters being used to avoid the problems caused by some characters, such as quote marks, in the course of electronic transfer of data. It is also possible that the everyday convention of capital letters at the beginning of sentences can further complicate matters as far as users are concerned. A button that just says *Back* as an abbreviation for "Go back" may not be immediately understood in that way, in particular by non-native speakers; this is something that merits further research.

Click here for help is potentially different than *Click here for Help* (with a capital H), if there is a special Help facility signaled by the capital letter. But on seeing *Click here for help* (with a small "h") elsewhere in the system, will the user recognize that this *help* is not the same as *Help*? Conventions need to be communicated to users. Still, that may not be enough—in addition, other visual means or verbal context can be used to remove ambiguity (e.g., "Click here for help with this task"). Capital letters used throughout a word make it convey loudness, so *Click here for HELP* invites a cry for help!

Krol (1994) describes the "tin" newsreader software that has a *quit* option in every command menu—the user must type *q* to quit. In this software, *quit* means "exit the current operation, and go to the next higher level." To go all the way to the top level, one must press *q* repeatedly or just *Q* (capital letter) once. It is easy for the user to make a mistake in this kind of choice, which depends on using the correct case. Hopefully, in the future this kind of problem can be avoided, but the need for explanation (what does it mean to *quit* this application?) is a fundamental one that will remain with us always.

The Allure of Short Forms and Acronyms

In chapter 1 we hinted at a comparison between words like *view* and *look at* in terms of one being shorter than the other. There are many reasons why we might need or want to opt for shorter forms of language, including convenience, convention, constraints of space, frequent repetition of a word, speed of communication, visual appeal, and precision.

Carroll (1985) has explored various naming strategies such as might be used for file name creation, including truncation (*arith* for *arithmetic*), contraction (*guidesht* for *guidesheet*), and blending (*checkit* for *check it*). Writing at a time when graphical interfaces were not yet in widespread use as they are today, he says that names for commands need to be easy to type and must therefore comprise few characters. Today, it is still the case that in many systems, commands consist of just one letter. As an example, Mosaic's commands available through keyboard shortcuts (Krol 1994, p. 320) are represented by letters: A (which stands for Annotate and means pop up the Annotate screen);

B (which stands for Back and means go back to the previous document), and so on. In everyday language, the most favored form of abbreviation are *acronyms*—pronounceable names formed of initial letters or of parts of words (e.g., *Oxfam* or *radar*). They are popular precisely because they can be treated and spoken like words.

When listed alphabetically in an index, however, the meaning of abbreviations is typically obscured—*FAQs* (frequently asked questions) would be listed under F, when they should also be listed under Q for questions. Reordering of elements (e.g., in file names): *featex* = e_xtract_fe_atures_ (Carroll 1985) can make it difficult to guess the meaning. At other times, it is a matter of knowing how to pronounce an abbreviation, for instance *VIP* is not pronounced as a word. Abbreviations and acronyms can be a shortcut to communication or a barrier. An abbreviation with no punctuation can inadvertently suggest another word, for instance *cap* (capital letter): a cap; *act* (active): to act; *pass* (passive): to pass. Nonnative speakers have extra difficulties with abbreviations for reasons of pronunciation and because abbreviations tend to be part of informal usage or very specific settings (e.g., the meaning of *Re:* on a memo or message).

Words that Matter

Can words like *Switch* or *Zoom* stand on their own in the interface? We have already noted (chapter 7) that there are words that carry a grammatical meaning, and these include prepositions: *at, for, from, in, with*, and so on. They are typically small words, which can give the impression that they can be omitted without penalty. *Switch* goes with *on, off, from*; *Zoom* goes with *in* or *out*, however. Words taken out of their grammatical framework have to rely on other contextual clues for conveying their meaning, which can lead to a great deal of guesswork on the part of users. Is *Empty folder* a statement about a folder or a command to empty the folder? In English, the articles *the, a, an* do have an effect on meaning. In some other languages they can change meaning completely.

Associations of nouns with verbs and adjectives can make a significant difference. Does *Notes* mean note-making (writing down own ideas, planning) or note-taking (recording what someone has said or written)? In the world of computing, where meanings change all the time, we cannot assume familiar collocations for words, either. What kinds of things can you *post*? What can you *subscribe to*? What can you *submit*? The answers are always changing. An electronic debate can be *clustered around a topic*, contributions to it can be *named* or *anonymous*, tagged as "agree" or "disagree"—all very different to what happens in a conventional debate, which means that the new words associated with a debate really matter for understanding the new meaning of "debate."

Because verbs like to be located with their objects, problems arise when they are not. In Word 6.01, the *View* menu contains *Header* and *Footer*. It allows you to *create a header or footer*, but you cannot *create a footnote* in the same View menu; you can only view an existing one (creating footnotes is done in the *Insert* menu). Do users notice the heading of the menu they are in? If words that matter to each other are not close together, users' understanding will be impaired.

NINE

Explanation and Assistance

The Concepts of Familiarity and Simplicity

It is easy to say that an explanation should be simple and that it should be written in familiar language. Advice of this sort is offered in many a technical writing handbook, often with limited elaboration. The concepts of familiarity and simplicity are not as straightforward as they appear to be, however. Users' familiarity with particular terms can never really be predetermined because of the different ways we can "know" a word (as described in chapter 2). And what exactly is "simple" language?

Hartley (1985), in his book on designing instructional text, makes several references to a writer's conscious selection of words for a target text. *Word length* is mentioned (short, familiar words are easier to understand, although some long words, because of their frequent use, are quite familiar, e.g., "communication"), *word type* (concrete words and phrases are clearer than abstract ones), and *ambiguity* resulting from excessive use of abbreviations and acronyms. He also writes about the option of using *readability formulas* to check the suitability of a text for a given reader age group. Emden (1990) devotes a section to vocabulary choice in her handbook on writing for engineers and offers this advice: "Use words which the reader will understand" (p. 22). She rightly points out the insidious danger in the use of technical language: "The reader may assume that he understands and the writer may assume that he is understood. Both may be understanding different meanings" (p. 18). Sides (1984), cautioning about the use of jargon in papers and reports on computer technology, says this: "The issue of jargon is audience-dependent. Always use what the audience will understand" (p. 5). This is sound advice, yet on reflection, it is so cursory that it is doubtful whether it can genuinely be followed. The writer can strive to get to know the audience, and even think about providing definitions of terms, but there is still the matter of knowing how to select words or adapt one's "jargon." Use "fewer and simpler words," advises Sides, referring to S. T. Coleridge as an authority on the matter. The problem is that knowing which words are simpler is not easy, and using fewer words can lead to not using enough!

Cutts (1996) offers a Plain English lexicon in which "official" terms are given "shorter, simpler and more conversational" alternatives. It includes words like *herewith* and *notwithstanding*, often found in legal language. The basis for recommending one word in favor of another is the knowledge that some words are used much more frequently in the language than others (statistical data are now available thanks to the existence of large electronic collections of texts). A small selection from this lexicon is shown in Table 4, featuring words that may be relevant to language in the user interface. Although the basic principle of simplification is one that we must take into consideration when developing an approach to explanations, the context of this particular Plain English advice on swapping words must be taken into account. The advice is directed at people who write official documents that are to be read by members of the general public. The situation is in some ways similar to communication with inexperienced computer users, but the difference is that a large proportion of the "official" terms are also technical ones, that is to say, they have very specific meanings in computing. The principle here is to review one's use of these terms in the user interface, checking to see whether their special meaning matters—whether they can be replaced. If they

Table 4. A sample of words from
the Plain English lexicon

Official terms	Plainer alternatives
additional	more, extra
assist	help
calculate	work out
category	group
component	part
disconnect	cut off
discontinue	stop, end
facilitate	help
failure to	if you do not
initiate	begin, start
in order to	to
principal	main, chief
prioritize	rank
prior to	before
sufficient	enough
terminate	end, stop
utilize	use
verify	check, prove

cannot, and that will often be the case, plainer alternatives can usually still be incorporated into explanations of specialized terms and into user-oriented indexes and other retrieval mechanisms. Barry (1993) lists some "polysyllabic terms to substitute for more mundane words" (p. 96) if you want to survive in the computer industry: for *make* use *generate*, for *functions* use *functionality*, for *method* use *methodology*—you get the picture.

Explaining Dangerous and Duplicated Actions

It has never been easy to find satisfactory ways of dealing with the definition of words and terms outside of the category of nouns. For example, formal, analytical methods are much better suited to nouns than they are to verbs. In both general and specialized language dictionaries, we are used to finding verbs explained by reference to synonyms or examples of use. However, explanations in a user interface (e.g., in its help facility or glossary) need to be rather different. This is due to the nature of the verbs and adjectives that particularly need to be explained, many of which refer to actions that are (potentially or actually) dangerous or ones that are duplicated.

We are using *dangerous actions* as a global term for actions that can lead to problems if misunderstood or misapplied or which may be worrying for users. Invisible objects such as *annotations* or *bookmarks* in a document can cause problems if their status is not obvious (e.g., does a bookmark become part of a text, and if so, can users *search* for it as they would for a word in the text?) Automatic processes can take users unaware, if they do not know in advance that they will happen (e.g., automatic spelling correction) and cannot find out about them easily when beginning to use a new application. Box 25 gives examples of verbs and adjectives that need to be treated with special care. Actions can be dangerous if they sound positive or reassuring but contain hidden dangers (i.e., they are deceptive). Invisible operations, such as copying something to a temporary file or *clipboard*, can be troublesome or alarming for users. Box 26 shows examples of potentially deceptive verbs and adjectives.

In a sense, practically any action is dangerous if the user has not understood its full implications. Choosing a *format* (*layout*, *style*, etc.) can be dangerous if one does not know whether it can be changed subsequently and how. Contrary to common sense, doing something for the first time can be easier than doing it again, because of new constraints (e.g., some data have been input and formatted, and the data must be preserved despite changes to its format!)

The main issue here is the possibility of anticipation of the effects of one's actions. There are a number of aspects to this:

1. *What comes first?* If, as a user, I want to do something in an application, I need to know about possible prerequisites (e.g., to create a *style*

Box 25. Words referring
to potentially dangerous
or worrying actions

in a word processor); do I need to have typed in some text first, to
which I will apply a style, or can I create a style without first having
typed in or chosen a text? This helps me to understand why some
actions appear to have no effect.

2. *What will be affected?* If I choose an option or button which says *hide*,
   for instance, what exactly will be hidden as a result? If there is no
   object following the word "hide" (it needs an object: to hide *something*), then an incorrect interpretation can take place. In applications
   that simulate books and notebooks and allow users to insert bookmarks, what are the effects of operations like *paste*, *copy*, or *move*
   on bookmarks?

sort	implies order, but can cause chaos
protect	can make something too inaccessible
save	it may be possible to overwrite
find	user may search but not find
add	can run out of space or memory
clear	may be destructive
fast	efficient, yet perhaps not as good as *slow*
new	*old* one may be discarded without warning
standard	may not be the best choice
complete	can be a matter of opinion or perception
copy	copied version may be invisible

Box 26. Deceptive words

3. *What will be happening at the same time?* Anticipation also depends on knowing about what happens automatically in the background, behind the scenes, while one is doing something else (e.g., *automatic saving* while one is typing, *updating* of a database while a form is filled in).
4. *When is the action complete?* An action may well involve a series of steps. *Delete* was mentioned as an example of this in chapter 6, but many more verbs fall into this category. Users need to know, and perhaps be reminded, that all steps must be performed in order, so that the action will be complete. That awareness is also necessary if they are asked to confirm that they have completed an action.
5. *Can it be undone?* In many cases, it is important to know whether an action is reversible and how it may be reversed (e.g., if I customize a screen or a menu, can I later go back to its original version? How easy is that to do?)

As an actual example of the last aspect, in Microsoft Word (6.0), a "Tip of the day" is offered to users each time the application is opened. For users, this can be a good way of continually adding to their knowledge. One such tip says: "You can quickly remove commands or other items from menus by pressing . . . [*a sequence of keys*]. Open a menu, and then choose the command or item you want to remove." The problem is that this advice can sound worrisome to a user who does not already know how to reverse the action, that is, how to get the removed commands back into the menu in the future, if needed.

A second issue is raised by what might be called *duplicated actions*, as that is how they can appear to users—it is about making explicit the difference between words that seem to have the same meanings. *Cut* resembles *delete* for instance. Singer (1995) reports in a usability study that some people experienced a certain amount of confusion between the functions *close* and *back* in a system where both terms designated an action of returning to a previous screen. Box 27 shows more sets of action words of this kind. Box 28 gives some pairs of nouns designating facilities or features with similar meanings.

stop	cancel	
choose	select	
search	find	go to
cut	delete	clear
close	back	quit

Box 27. Similar actions: How obvious are the differences between them?

note	annotation
headings	outline
box	frame
picture	drawing
clipboard	spike
table	spreadsheet

Box 28. Facilities and features
that appear similar

Formal, Informal, and Jargon-Free Definitions

It is well known that formal definitions of terms, important as they are from the points of view of clarity and standardization, are not the most effective way of communicating knowledge to the general reader. Formality of structure as well as formality and specialization of vocabulary get in the way of ease of understanding. There are, of course, different tactics for overcoming these problems in definitions or, more loosely, in explanations. Readers who require a detailed account of the many different established methods of definition and description might like to look at a book such as Mills and Walter (1978), where the concept of an amplified definition is also explained. Briefly, *an amplified definition* is one that gives extra information in the form of concrete examples, comparisons, physical descriptions, basic underlying principles, causes and effects, explanation of a term's origin, further definitions of terms, and so on.

Encyclopedic dictionaries have always catered to the need for expanding on a definition, and encyclopedias fill a need for access to knowledge about names, events, and places, sometimes accompanied by anecdotes and illustrations. James Rutherford, Chief Education Officer at the American Association for the Advancement of Science, writing in the foreword to Brennan (1992), has this to say about definitions (emphasis added):

> . . . the clarity of the definitions must be superb. It also helps if the definitions are to the point and *intriguing enough to cause us to sample new terms at random* after locating the answer to our initial query.

The dictionary in question is a work of reference intended for the "intelligent nonscientist" who reads science articles in the press. So, a definition in this type of work should not only communicate the meaning of the term being looked up but also draw the reader in, arousing an interest in the subject. The dictionary's author, Richard Brennan, describes his approach (emphasis added):

Each entry consists of a concise definition *followed by a sentence or two* relating the technical term to something in our daily lives or expanding on the concise definition in some way to make it *more easily understandable or memorable*. I call this approach *Definition +*. (p. xiii)

"Definition +" can be exemplified by an entry from the same dictionary, shown in Box 29. This example certainly fulfills the criteria described by Brennan. Is it also "intriguing enough to cause us to sample new terms at random after locating the answer to our initial query," as required by Rutherford? That is difficult to answer, as each reader will have a different personal response and motivation. But we can usefully ask a similar question: "Will it cause us to sample new terms—related terms, not random ones—after locating the answer?" The cross-references are one well established and proven method of prompting further reading and helping readers to build their understanding. However, in this example, if a reader wanted to find out more about cooking methods, for instance, or about chocolate, the search would be much more difficult, perhaps disappointing, because the dictionary is deliberately very selective in its coverage. This type of constraint inevitably affects all such reference works to some degree. A reader's appetite is whetted, but then it cannot be satisfied.

So the amplified definition, or "Definition +" in this incarnation, can be used as a way of overcoming the forbidding nature of the traditional, formal definition. Gookin et al. (1993) takes a startlingly different approach, with a very casual, jargon-free, and often flippant approach to explanations. Their factual accuracy is sometimes a matter for the reader's judgment:

Microwave:

- An electromagnetic wave of extremely high frequency.
- A microwave oven uses these high-frequency waves to penetrate and heat food. Microwaves heat materials by vibrating the bonds between ATOMS, causing friction; the resulting HEAT causes food to cook in a relatively short time.
- The phenomenon of microwave cooking was discovered by accident when a scientist doing some research involving microwaves discovered that a chocolate bar in his shirt pocket had melted and [he] began to investigate.

Box 29. An example of "Definition +" from the *Dictionary of Scientific Literacy* (Brennan 1992). (Note: words in capitals are cross-references in the dictionary.)

> *documentation* = The fat instruction manuals that everyone pays
> money for but no-one bothers to read. Usually full of instructions
> that don't work, don't make sense, or are just plain wrong.

This dictionary is fairly unusual among special subject dictionaries in having, for each dictionary entry, a sentence that illustrates the term's usage; for
instance, for the term *pagination*:

> If I can't figure out how the *pagination* works in my word pro-
> cessing program, I'll have to print my novel as one long scroll.

A more traditional approach is to describe, rather than illustrate, usage,
through expressions like "the term is used for . . . ," "this is done by . . . ,"
"this technique is used in . . . ," such as:

> *Diagnose*—To determine the nature of a problem with a computer sys-
> tem by examining the effects of the problem. *The term is more often
> used for hardware problems*, while *debug* is more commonly used for
> software problems. (Stokes 1985; emphasis added)

As a rule, illustrative sentences are an excellent complement to a definition. In Gookin et al. (1993) mentioned above, many of the sentences are
humorous; it is likely that some people will find them patronizing (the title
of the dictionary—*The Illustrated Computer Dictionary for Dummies*—should
have been sufficient warning, however!); for instance, for *relational operator*:

> I used a *relational operator* to calculate whether meat loaf was
> better than sushi for dinner tonight.

A lighthearted tone is quite often adopted in user guides. Ron Mansfield"s
definitions in *Windows 95 for Busy People* are, as the author says, "informal,
and often a little playful" (p. xxii). For example:

> *Windows 95 shortcut icon* = Little picture of a folder, printer, com-
> puter, or other resource. With any luck, these rascals remember the
> original item's location. Double-clicking or otherwise selecting a short-
> cut icon takes you to the actual item without a lot of rummaging. (Too
> bad these don't work on wooden desktops too. . . .) (1996, p. 184)

Humor is certainly more acceptable in independent dictionaries and user
guides than in official manuals or in on-screen definitions, because the author is at a distance from the software. Apart from humor, there are other
psychological ways of taking the tension out of an explanation, as can be seen
in these examples from the informal dictionary of computer terms by Williams and Cummings (1993) (emphasis added):

Database = A database is *just* a collection of information stored in computerized form. The *simplest* way to understand a database is to think of it like a set of 3x5 cards. . . .

Macro = A macro is a programmed shortcut, programmed by *you, to make life at your computer easier.*

To round off this section on definition styles and lead us into the next one on structures, it is worth mentioning that jargon can be avoided to some extent by demonstrating meanings in a visual way. Many recent user guides on computer applications take this approach. For instance, Maran (1994) uses full color illustrations on every page as a technique of "simplification" and partial avoidance of the jargon problem.

The Structure of Explanations

Word 4.0 balloon help on the Macintosh offers the following explanation of the "Create publisher" option in its *Edit* menu:

Create publisher—Creates a publisher containing the selection in your document

This is a definition with a circular structure (the word being defined is itself used in the definition), and it leads us to consider what are the different structures that may be used in formulating explanations. A traditional definition for a word begins with a *classifier* (the name of a general category, or class, to which the word belongs) and contains some information that allows us to distinguish the word from other words in the same category. For example, a house is "a building for human habitation" (Brown 1983). This approach is good, but it is not suitable for every word in every situation. In particular, the formal vocabulary used in traditional definitions is difficult for learners of a language, and special dictionaries have been developed for learners.

Sinclair (1991) sets forth his philosophy with regard to the language of explanation by describing the definition structures developed on the Cobuild English language dictionary project, which has language learners as its main target audience. He introduces it like this:

In the later stages of compiling the Cobuild dictionary, . . . it was decided to develop a new style of presenting lexicographical information. The process began in a straightforward attempt to explain the meaning and use of words in ordinary English sentences, and it ended in a radical critique of conventional lexicography. This exercise now appears to be the first step in articulating a theory of language reflexiv-ity—the capacity of language to talk about itself. (p. 123)

Some statements from the Cobuild dictionary given by Sinclair show how explanations can be formulated for different parts of speech:

A *house*	is a building in which people live
If you *defeat* someone	you win a victory over them in a contest
If someone *totters*	they walk in an unsteady way
A *pure* substance	is not mixed with anything else
If something happens *often*	it happens many times or much of the time

Each word in italic type is the "topic" of the sentence, and the rest of the first part is the "co-text"; the second part of each sentence is an explanatory "com-ment" on the topic. A detailed analysis of the structure of these explanations can be found in Sinclair (1991). This way of writing definitions is becoming ever more popular and can be applied in specialized subject fields. As an example, software programs need to be explained by reference to their *function*, and the following definition does just that:

> *Shareware* allows prospective software buyers to evaluate a wide vari-ety of software free of charge. Having decided the software is suitable, the purchaser must pay the software author a nominal fee for the right to use it. (Hatley 1996)

Research carried out by Paris (1988) showed that depending on a user's assumed level of expertise, a description of an object could be either *parts-oriented* or *process-oriented*. Experienced users already understood pro-cesses, so they mainly needed to know about an object's subparts (its struc-ture) and properties, whereas the less experienced needed to know how parts work together to achieve an object's function. Levels of expertise could be determined partly by studying the questions that users asked, such as "Does this disk drive have three bearings?" as opposed to "What is a disk drive?"

Williams and Cummings (1993) give an explanation of the term *file con-version* by first saying why the concept is needed and then what the process in question involves:

> *File conversion*: Not all software applications can read documents created in other applications, so sometimes you have to do a file conversion to convert one file into a file format that another ap-plication can read.

This approach is helpful in building understanding. If we know something more about users, we can also link new ideas to their prior knowledge and to their previous understanding of meanings. Explanations are a means of building confidence, which is a by-product of growth in certain types of knowledge, especially:

- knowledge of behavior and properties of objects
- extent of one's control over those objects
- possible effects of actions, scope of actions
- procedures and actions admissible within the application
- events occurring within the application

The way in which language patterns (verbs with nouns, nouns with adjectives, etc.) relate to objects, actions, and their properties in a new type of dictionary of electronic spreadsheet terminology for translators is shown in Kukulska-Hulme and Knowles (1989) and in Kukulska-Hulme (1990b).

The conceptual structure of explanations can sometimes be enhanced through visual means such as typography and layout. A definition of *tele-learning* by Collis (1996), based on a "what-where-how-why" structure, is presented like this (each part of the definition is later amplified):

> Tele-learning is:
> making connections
> among persons and resources
> through communication technologies
> for learning-related purposes

People new to a subject area particularly appreciate information presented in a structured way. Tree structures, tables of decisions and alternatives, even good use of paragraphs, can make orientation easier within a subject area. Pictures and diagrams have always been used in encyclopedic reference works and in illustrated dictionaries to promote understanding. Animations are a breakthrough for computer-based explanation systems and can be used to show actions, processes, and events, as well as revealing the way in which parts of a whole fit together, or are built up, layer upon layer.

What Kinds of Assistance Do Users Need?

As any computer user knows, a help system is not enough to turn a hostile interface into a user-friendly one. Nonetheless, help is important. "No interactive system of any complexity is so intuitive that the user never requires help. Help should therefore be an integral part of the design" (Dix et al. 1993,

p. 419). How is help to become integrated into the design? The message that should be coming across in this book is that help should become integral through *helpful language* in the user interface: That is the best way to tackle this problem. Helpful language must also feature in help facilities—but these cannot be "thrown in" to counteract the harmful effects of a hostile or perplexing user interface. Some users have had such bad experiences with help facilities that they now refuse to look at them in any new application (Kukulska-Hulme 1996b).

When, as a user, you are looking at an application for the first time, you need to understand the options on the screen to get a feel for the range of facilities being offered. When you are looking to perform a particular task, you want help that will allow you to complete the task quickly. Another type of help—and this one is often overlooked—should make it possible for users to understand the application more fully so that the best ways of meeting users' needs in various situations can be found, something that the application program alone cannot be expected to do in a fully intelligent way. Training normally tries to address this point, but self-training is becoming ever more popular. What is more, there is no reason why "best" ways of using an application should be something that you find out in due course—to you as a user, it is perhaps the most important aspect of application use and one that you would want to grasp immediately. An analogy with foreign language learning that can be brought out here is that we normally want to learn very early on how to cope in various situations, such as what is the best way of asking for a discount or the best way to make a complaint or get relevant information quickly.

In many current applications, to find out about the best ways of using a system one has to think in terms of words like *optimize* or *customize*. Surely users are not thinking, "How do I optimize my performance?" but rather "What's the quickest/easiest/simplest/most secure/most flexible way to do this?" User guides deal with the issue to some extent by providing "how-to" instructions, lists of shortcuts, or timesaving tips and techniques [e.g., in Mansfield (1996), the latter are called "Habits and Strategies"], but this is not quite enough. The way forward is to allow quicker and more accurate understanding of the specialized language of the interface, so that users can judge for themselves what is the best way of tackling a particular task. It is also important to incorporate users' everyday language patterns into retrieval mechanisms such as indexes.

It is useful to distinguish between *functional help* in any application (dealing with questions such as: What is the effect of this command? What is the difference between these options? How do I get out of here?) and *task* or *study help*, which might deal with instructions, strategies, concepts, objectives, recommendations, and lists of names or codes—according to the type of system in question. Help systems that do not require users to think at all, because they are taken step-by-step through a sequence of actions or manipulations in a foolproof way, are limiting in the long run. They encourage dependency and so do not help users to become autonomous. Demonstrations of actions and results are extremely valuable for building up users' mental models, but ultimately, if the steps to follow are reasonably complex, they must be understood.

Because help facilities are not normally the most visible part of applications, they do tend to be neglected and may display an inconsistent interface, which changes depending on when and how they are consulted and is therefore confusing for users.

Choice of Words for Psychological Support

There are many different words that convey the idea of "help" in the English language. Box 30 shows a fair selection of such words, some of them figurative, along with some that refer to people capable of giving help or advice. The terms all have different values (as discussed in chapter 5), and the purpose of bringing them together is to facilitate a comparison of their values and possible effects on users. "Help" is a general term, which potentially covers many meanings. In some applications, qualified "help" (e.g., *study help*), a more specific word, or a helper role word may be more appropriate. In a recent series of trials of new educational software at the Open University, some users reported an aversion to the help function based purely on negative past experience of help in commercial applications (as mentioned above), so finding an alternative description could be important. Thinking aloud during testing, they were heard to say things such as "What do I do now? I suppose I could try pressing Help. . . ." But instead, after a moment's hesitation, they turned to other options on the screen and to general experimentation, with various consequences.

instructions	tutorial	guide	monitor
assistance	notes	teacher	mentor
advice	suggestions	adviser	agent
hints	clues	technician	assistant
prompts	start here	counselor	doctor
warnings	revision	expert	organizer
self-help	first aid	motivator	manager
recommendations	pep talk	planner	mediator
information	bail me out!	strategist	advocate
reminders	trouble-shooting	wizard	friend
support	what now?	tutor	muse

Box 30. Synonyms for "help" and "person who can help"

It is usual for someone to have to ask for help before it is given, but sometimes one gets help without asking. *Warnings* or *encouragement*, for instance, may be given without asking, which is not to say that one should not be able to ask for them. It is inevitable that through language an application will display a certain personality to its users, helpful or otherwise [as noted by Newton (1991)].

In the previous chapter on explanations, we saw how language was being used to remove anxiety and tension through words like *just, simplest, making life easier*. Box 31 gives further suggestions of words and phrases that are likely—though not guaranteed—to have a reassuring or supportive effect on users. There is, of course, a thin line, which must not be crossed, between this type of language and the language of selling and advertizing, which can be perceived as irritating, insulting, or patronizing by users.

Help in Orientation and Retrieval

From a user's perspective, the language of orientation within a system is largely informal in character. Singer (1995) recounts that students' queries noted during the use of an educational piece of software were "invariably of the forms 'How do I do this?', 'What do I do next?', and 'Where do I go from here?'" (p. 15). Questions concerning orientation and navigation, as shown in Box 32, can cover:

- following tracks and links
- searching for something specific
- progression in stages through structured learning
- browsing
- movement through time
- seeking an overview
- evaluating importance

convenient	reliable
achievable	workable
practical	easily managed
secure	safe
definite	dependable
insures against	works well
gives scope for	without difficulty
made easier	save yourself trouble
made possible	take a shortcut

Box 31. Language that reassures and supports users

What now?	How do I get there?
What next?	How do I get back?
What did I just do?	How do I get out of here?
Where am I?	What parts are there?
Where is it?	How many are there?
Where does this belong?	How much more is there?
Is this the same place?	How long will it take?
Is this the main place?	How long did it take?

Box 32. Sample of questions for orientation and navigation

A user-centered approach to information retrieval also takes users' questions as a starting point. It has been said that "as a necessary condition to satisfying the need to obtain information, we must be able to formulate our informational needs" (Wessel 1975, p. 4). The ability to formulate needs in the form of questions is a skill that can be developed (Kukulska-Hulme 1988b), and it is also the most widespread everyday way of obtaining information. We normally obtain information in order to do something with the knowledge gained—to act in an informed way. If we recognize that retrieval is related to subsequent action, this may be sufficient grounds to cast doubt on the prevalent tendency in information retrieval facilities to favor nouns over other parts of speech. There are good reasons for it when one is dealing with the problem of matching retrieval terms to terms in a body of specialized texts. But when we shift the focus from text to user, we are faced with the possibility that needs might be centered on verbs (and other parts of speech) if they are concerned with action.

This is tied to the important point that access mechanisms such as indexes, tables of contents, and help facilities, need to be designed at the same time as other aspects of a user interface or a set of documentation—they should not be an afterthought. Indexes merit special consideration. In a user-oriented set of indexes, a distinction can be made between instructions, understanding of concepts, advice on best practice, and information about who is in control of various operations. A link should be established between users' language and the specialized language of the application. This means that apart from specialized terms, other words should be included (within their usual patterns: adjectives with nouns and so on), especially:

- abstract notions from the general language (e.g., words such as *difference, method, rationale, limits, advantages*)
- notions of timing and manner (e.g., *frequency, steps, ways*)
- high-level concepts from the application area in question (e.g., *check, backup, damage*)

- colloquial or general language synonyms for specialized verbs (e.g., *leave, change, get rid of, see, keep, find out*)
- adjectives and adverbs: (e.g., *lost, potential, available, remotely, regularly*)
- words expressing possibility, advisability, necessity (e.g., *possible, necessary, feasible, constraints*)

Compiling an index half way through writing a document can help an author to determine what should be the content of the document and to become aware of terminological choices. It will show multiple terms being used for the same concept, different adjectives being attached to a noun and subtly altering its meaning as the text progresses. It can be a way of checking what has been said about a topic so far; it will also show up gaps in coverage. Most importantly, it can force an author to think about intended readers, their expectations, and their needs.

IV

SUMMARY AND RECOMMENDATIONS

TEN

Making It Work

This chapter summarizes the main points of the communicative approach to user interface and documentation design. The term "designer" is used here to refer to anyone who designs and develops a user interface or writes user documentation.

As stated at the beginning, the main ambition of this book is to further our understanding of the *nature* of the problems observed and to establish the language *concepts* (rather than guidelines) that will help designers when thinking about solutions to problems. Of course, the practical side is very important and must be further developed by those whose job it is to create design methodologies, standards, and guidelines. The present chapter highlights elements of practical advice given in earlier chapters and states the implications of what has been said. Accordingly, the style of presentation is different: everything is contained in bullet lists. It is assumed that previous chapters have been read, or will be read, as the supporting arguments are not developed here. The view expressed by Smith (1990) seems fitting:

> Guidelines cannot replace task analysis. Indeed many guidelines, when considered along with their associated commentary, imply the need for careful task analysis to determine design requirements. Guidelines will not necessarily save work in user interface design, but in fact may entail extra work, at least in the initial stage of establishing design rules. If that initial work is well done, however, then subsequent software design should be more efficient and, of course, should produce a better user interface. (p. 887)

What needs to be added is that the initial stage that comprises audience and task analysis [e.g., as described by Bradford (1988) and Brockmann (1986)] must include language requirements analysis if successful communication with users is envisaged in the interface.

Key Aspects of the Communicative Approach

- The concept of *computer literacy* creates a barrier to effective communication—*people literacy* and *language literacy* are much better concepts to work with.
- Communication is *language in action*: Both spoken and written language must be seen in this light.
- Communication involves people, which means that its *cultural, social,* and *psychological contexts* must be considered.
  - The *cultural contexts* that matter most are the technological world view, which may not be shared by designers and users, and also the particular cultural connotations and references made through language.
  - The *social context* determines the part that users play or do not play in establishing the meanings of the words in the interface to the applications they have to use and the relationship of the application to their professional concerns.
  - The *psychological context* of communication is made up of users' intentions, expectations, presumptions, and inferences, as well as states such as fear or antagonism and feelings of enjoyment or confidence.
- We have to find out about *how people use their language* before we can be sure that what we say or write on the screen and in printed documentation will be understood by them.
- There is a difference between *not understanding* and *misunderstanding*: Users who do not understand become frustrated and powerless; users who misunderstand waste time and create problems.
- Language used in a way that is not matched to the *purpose of communication* in a given situation is inappropriate, and will fail to have the desired effect on users.
- Technological advancements create new communication environments that call for new meanings and new forms; in some applications we have to communicate to users something of the *nature of the environment* as well as just giving its functions.

Reviewing Designers' Skills and Training Needs

- The ideal designer of an interactive application—or the ideal team—will have expertise in many different subjects, but one of these will definitely be the field of *language and communication*.

- Designers need to *know and feel confident about* using the specialized language of this field, its terminology, and phraseology, and to be able to work with the concepts it offers.
- *The ability to foresee or imagine* the effects of language in use, to foresee the communicative acts in which users will be involved, the ability to specify the purpose of communication and to anticipate problems, and the ability to think through the implications of introducing language change—all these have to be developed.
- Designers need to be aware of strategies and mechanisms in language that promote good communication, such as *coherence, cohesion,* and *redundancy.*
- Language specialists invited to offer advice on user interface design should have appropriate expertise in the *communicative approach to language;* communicative language teaching is a prime example of the type of expertise required.
- The potential problems of *nonnative speakers of English* have to be appreciated where that is relevant to the application. Contact with professional translators or teachers can be most helpful, as they have expert knowledge of contrasts and areas of difficulty between languages and of the different structures used in each language to convey the same meaning.
- *Methods of capturing and analyzing users' language* must be taught to members of a design team—methods such as think-aloud protocol analysis, setting up a corpus of written texts and transcribed speech interactions, and ways of building on the results.
- Guidance on language and communication principles should be incorporated into *documents that deal with standards and guidelines* for designers and developers.
- Working methods need to be reviewed, such that *indexes* and *other retrieval aids* can be developed in parallel with help text and user documentation, rather than at the end of a project, and their style and location can be adapted.
- Reference material based on an index of words used in a particular design environment, at operating system level and in previous applications and documentation, should be made available to *designers of subsequent applications.*
- Methods of *recording reasons for selection of terms* in the user interface should be developed in environments where translation into foreign languages is envisaged, along with methods of specifying differences of meaning between candidate terms.

Understanding and Involving Users

- Users should be seen as *language learners,* because any new application environment puts them in a language learning situation; learning should be encouraged and helped along by appropriate facilities within an application.

- Understanding users begins with describing the *personal, social,* and *cultural contexts* in which they operate.
- On a more detailed level, it involves knowing their *needs* and *intentions,* as expressed through questions they might have about an application and the predominant concerns in their particular domain or situation.
- It also involves looking at *users' perceptions of meanings:* the prior knowledge they bring to their understanding, the effects on meaning produced by context of use, the perceived values of words, the effort of imagination required in order to understand a given piece of text, and awareness of which application or module is running.
- *Prior knowledge* that users bring to a new application includes knowledge about the meanings of words in other situations (e.g., in everyday conversation, in other areas of specialization), knowledge of word patterns in other contexts, incomplete knowledge, and various associations that may or may not be relevant.
- Involving users at the early stages of design is crucial, inviting them to specify their *requirements in terms of help and support* within the application, giving them some suggestions as to what is possible; this gives users a constructive role alongside the more mundane role of specifying functional requirements and the critical role that entitles them to say how the system falls short of meeting their requirements.
- It is also about inviting users to *participate in decisions about the language* that will be used in the interface, having narrowed down the possibilities beforehand in terms of important design constraints.
- Users should not feel that designers are the "authority" on all aspects of design, including language, but instead should be encouraged to *appropriate an application by identifying with its language;* users need to feel that they are not outsiders with respect to the technological culture.

Recognizing Speech in Writing

- Interactive applications create a *special environment for written language,* one in which written technical communication takes on the human and social dimensions normally associated with spoken language.
- At the same time, there is no immediate feedback in written communication—as designers and developers, we may never know that we failed to communicate. It is possible to *capture user feedback on language* at the stage of developmental testing, if we are interested in getting that information and using it to improve the system.
- In the language system, *speech and writing are not completely separable;* it is true that some forms of language are rarely, if ever, written, and vice versa, but it is also true that whatever is spoken can be written down, and what is written is normally read aloud or silently.
- Language on the screen should therefore be *read out loud,* not just individual words, but sequences arising from juxtaposed words and resulting

from selections of options; the reading might also bring up some linking words absent from the interface, giving an opportunity to assess their potential value to the user.

- *Variations in intonation* would also be worth trying, given that features of sound can change meaning; this can be a way of detecting missing punctuation.
- *Words that sound alike*, heard by users in conversation or in training, might be confused when seen in writing, and their spelling might not be known; this must be considered in the design of retrieval or access mechanisms in the user interface.

Making Text Understandable

- Every piece of text, even if it only consists of one or two words, should be written with a *clear purpose* in mind; the purpose must be matched to users' needs and must determine the choice of language variety and style.
- Synonyms must be managed: their purpose has to be clearly understood by designers, and they must either be eliminated from the interface or justified to users; synonyms in retrieval aids must include *nontechnical words and phrases*.
- Language varieties to be included in the interface must be examined: *consistency* within a variety and *clear boundaries* between varieties are two principles to follow; users' familiarity with the varieties must be considered.
- The *meanings of terms* in any application always have to be explained, because they are highly likely to be unique to that application: even the meanings of the most straightforward terms like *help*, *open*, or *cancel* cannot be assumed.
- Explanations help users to become aware of the fact that their language is changing and to feel that they have *a degree of control* over that process.
- Users' ability to understand an explanation is dependent on its precision, so explanations must not be vague; it helps if explanations *show relationships between similar and related terms*.
- Explanations do not have to be phrased in the same *variety or style of language* as that used in the application or operating system interface; for example, the variety could be more informal, the style could be more metaphorical. (But the needs of any nonnative speakers may need to be borne in mind.)
- Understanding is a process that involves the building and rebuilding of *mental models*; we have to help users in that process, by providing better information about meanings—behaviors of objects, possible events, sequences of events, attributes, and so on (but not using such language!), and by helping to remove possible misapprehensions.
- *Grammatical words* are essential for communication; they should not be stripped from the language for no reason.
- When there is *no room on the screen* to display more words or more text,

alternative techniques should be considered, such as labels that appear when you point to an option or button.

Equipping Users for Communication

- New application environments put users in a situation where they do not necessarily have the lexical resources to express what they mean—they have to *learn new words and meanings.*
- Users must be helped to acquire the language of a new application in such a way that they are able to *use it productively* to communicate with the application; they should move beyond understanding, to productive use—being able to articulate their needs in the new language.
- This process of learning involves *initial contact* with words, *understanding,* and *personal experience* (which is repeated understanding and productive use).
- An essential aspect of learning new words is finding out *how they function in discourse*—when it is appropriate to use them and what their collocates are.
- Users need to build up *a repertoire of words and structures,* consisting of words related in meaning, on the same level of detail, and grouped according to grammatical category; for example, all of the verbs used to manipulate windows and all of the adjectives attached to document types.
- Equipping users to *talk about metaphors* that figure in the user interface is part of ensuring that they can be used effectively.

Designing for Nonnative Speakers of English

- The special needs of *nonnative speakers of English* can be addressed by finding out about *areas of difficulty,* especially "false friends," terms not normally encountered in English language learning; phrasal verbs; different assumptions about meanings; and phrases requiring an "unpacking" effort.
- *Representatives of target nonnative speakers* should assist in design and developmental testing, one of their roles being to read aloud the words on the screen to check for possible misunderstanding based on mispronunciation, another being to advise on culturally and socially conditioned interpretations of meaning and on cases of genuine ambiguity (where two completely different meanings are possible).
- Certain aspects of interface design need to be treated with special caution, especially *metaphors* and *graphic symbols,* which may not be meaningful to all cultures; text can be used to clarify their meanings.
- *Writing styles* are specific to cultures rather than languages; some writing styles are impossible to translate and may hinder the translation process.
- Writing for possible translation into another language involves checking one's language for ambiguity and providing *extra verbal context* where possible.

- Translation can become easier if a limited, *controlled version* of the English language has been used.
- *Ultra short stretches of language* (e.g., one term, out of verbal context) are generally more difficult to translate than longer stretches.

Screen and Document: What Is Important

- Users' *ease of communication* should become a priority in interface design, such that it can shape design decisions at an early stage; *designers of operating systems* should be the first to take note.
- Sufficient verbal context must always be provided; sufficient context includes the provision of *complete and visible "patterns" of language*.
- It must be possible for users to quickly gain a full understanding of an application, so that they can adopt the *best ways of using it* without delay. If different ways of doing things exist, they must be explained, so that users can choose.
- Knowledge building can be facilitated through explicit links between concepts or terms related in a variety of ways—through *similarity of form*, not only meaning.
- *Areas of possible confusion* in language should be identified for a planned application; for example, confusion between computing terms and terms from a special subject area, terms in previously used applications, words that look or sound alike, and words with similar meanings.
- Access mechanisms such as lists of contents and indexes should contain *nontechnical terms* and *a variety of parts of speech*; headings should be informative.
- In menu options, it is better, where possible, to opt for *consistency in parts of speech* (e.g., a verb at the start of each option in a list).
- It is wise to allow for *fuzzy concepts* and for *modality*. "How do I . . . ?" is not the only question users ask, and it is normal for them not to be able to name things correctly.
- Since not all icons and graphic symbols will be understood, *text equivalents* should be readily available upon request.

Improving Access Mechanisms

- Access mechanisms (indexes, tables of contents, and help facilities) need to be designed *in parallel* with the development of a user interface or a set of documentation, not as an afterthought; the compilation of an index in the course of writing a document can help determine what should be the content of the document.
- Access mechanisms need to be designed to reflect users' needs in terms of *knowledge types* and *varieties of language*.

- For instance, in indexes, a distinction can be made between *instructions, understanding of concepts, advice on best practice*, and *information* about who is in control of various operations.
- The language used in indexes should include *abstract notions* from the general language, including notions of timing and manner, and *high-level concepts* from the application area in question, as a way of establishing a link between users' language and the specialized language of the application.
- *Terms* and *concepts from other domains* that have an impact on the comprehension of the main subject or application area should be included in the index; for instance, in relation to the domain of computer security, these could be business and legal terms.
- All parts of speech, not just nouns, are candidates for an index; *verbs* are important, not just verbs with specialized meanings, but their *synonyms in everyday language.*
- When they are listed alphabetically in an index, *the meaning of abbreviations* is typically obscured; for example, *FAQs* (frequently asked questions) are listed under F, when they should also be listed under Q for questions.
- Indexing principles should be explained to users, as *the meaning of the term "index" is not self-evident*; but the explanation should not be focused on technical aspects of indexing but on helping users get the most out of the index.
- *Multilevel indexing* is a possibility, where terms and knowledge types combine to show relevant information to users.

Research Needs: Users' Language and New Technologies

- There is a need for ongoing research into the *effects of new technologies on communication* and on interface design.
- One important area is experimental investigation of how the *mental lexicon of computing terms* is organized.
- Further work is needed to support and extend our knowledge of users' problems experienced at the interface to *applications involving speakers of different languages*, such as collaboration and distance learning.
- For example, it is possible that conventions in the use of capital letters compete with other *visual conventions* in user interface design and stand in the way of understanding.
- The relationship between *content words* and *function words* in the language of user interfaces needs to be examined closely to describe the tension between the pragmatic nature of an interface and the content words that are typically used to represent a system's functions.
- Although we know that *women's use of language* can be different from men's, we do not yet fully understand the implications of this for interface design.

Language Resources and Further Readings

This Appendix lists useful sources of information about language and communication in addition to those already mentioned in the main body of the book.

Searchable Collections of English Language Texts on the Web

These collections of texts (or "corpora") can be used to learn about usage of words or phrases in modern English. They are a means to better understanding users' prior knowledge and their expectations as to the meanings and behavior of particular words.

The British National Corpus (BNC)
(http://info.ox.ac.uk:80/bnc/)
   The British National Corpus is a collection of samples of written and spoken language from a wide range of sources, representing a wide cross-section of current British English. It is the joint effort of dictionary publishers (Oxford, Longman, Chambers-Harrap) and a number of academic research centers (Oxford University Computing Services, Unit for Computer Research in the English Language at Lancaster University, British Library Research and Development).

Collins COBUILD—Bank of English
(http://titania.cobuild.collins.co.uk/h)
   The Bank of English is a collection of samples of modern English for analysis of words, meanings, grammar, and usage. It is composed of a wide range

of written and oral specimens from many sources. Written texts come from newspapers, magazines, fiction and nonfiction books, brochures, leaflets, reports, and letters, while the spoken word is represented by transcriptions of everyday conversation, radio broadcasts, meetings, interviews, discussions. The majority of texts originate after 1990. The Bank of English was launched in 1991 by COBUILD (a division of HarperCollins Publishers) and The University of Birmingham. COBUILD, which is based within the School of English at Birmingham University, has been collecting a corpus of texts on computer since 1980 for dictionary compilation, language study, and the teaching of vocabulary and grammar.

A CobuildDirect Internet service allows direct connection to the computer system at Birmingham where the Bank of English is located.

Humanities Text Initiative at the University of Michigan
(http://www.hti.umich.edu/all/unrestrict.html)
"Unrestricted Resources" are accessible to anyone and can be searched online for words or phrases.

Center for Electronic Texts in the Humanities (CETH)
(http://www.ceth.rutgers.edu/)
The Center for Electronic Texts in the Humanities was established by Rutgers and Princeton Universities in 1991. The Web site includes a Directory of Electronic Text Centers and an overview of humanities computing.

The Electronic Text Library at the University of Virginia
(http://etext.lib.virginia.edu/uvaonline.html)
The Publicly Accessible part of the Modern English Collection is searchable; the electronic library also houses French, German, and Japanese texts.

The International Corpus of English (ICE)
(http://www.ucl.ac.uk/english-usage)
The International Corpus of English, coordinated by the Survey of English Usage at University College London, aims to provide material for comparative studies of the diversity of English throughout the world. Each participating country is collecting a corpus of one million words of their own national or regional variety of English, spoken or written between 1990 and 1996. ICE incorporates the International Corpus of Learner English (ICLE). This corpus samples the English used by advanced learners from ten different language backgrounds—French, Dutch, German, Spanish, Swedish, Finnish, Czech, Polish, Japanese, and Chinese.

Other Electronic Text Collections
There are many other well known collections of electronic texts; for example, Brown Corpus, Lancaster-Oslo/Bergen (LOB), London-Lund Corpus,

Lancaster Spoken English Corpus, Longman/Lancaster English Language Corpus, Kolhapur Corpus of Indian English, Computerized English Texts (COMET) for texts from Scottish sources, American Heritage Intermediate Corpus, Corpus of Spoken American English (CSAE), CallHome American English, Association for Computational Linguistics Data Collection Initiative (ACL/DCI), European Corpus Initiative (ACL/ECI), and Cambridge Language Survey (CLS).

Books Relevant to Text and Corpus Analysis
McCarthy, M. *Discourse Analysis for Language Teachers.* Cambridge Language Teaching Library, Cambridge University Press: Cambridge, 1991.
Sinclair, J. *Reading Concordances.* Longman: London, 1997.
Thomas, J., and Short, M., eds. *Using Corpora for Language Research.* Longman: London, 1996.
Stubbs, M. *Text and Corpus Analysis.* Blackwell: Oxford, 1996.

Directories of Language Resources on the Web

The Human-Languages Page
(http://www.june29.com/HLP/)
The Human-Languages Page is a catalog of language-related Internet resources, including on-line language lessons, dictionaries, translation services, language organizations, and lists of parallel texts in different languages.

The HUMBUL Gateway
International Resources for the Humanities: Language and Linguistics and Dictionaries and Reference Works (http://users.ox.ac.uk/~humbul/).
These HUMBUL pages list linguistics and languages resources available on the Web, including dictionaries. Languages covered include Arabic, Chinese, Finnish, French, Gaelic, German, Hindi, Italian, Russian, Spanish, Swedish, Thai, and Welsh.

English to Foreign Language Dictionaries of Common Computing Terms
(http://www.css.qmw.ac.uk/foreign/index.htm)
Simple alphabetical word lists with foreign language equivalents of computing terms.

Interactive Coursebook on the Web

Language and Learning Awareness—An Introduction to Teaching English as a Foreign Language
(http://www.edunet.com/nec/index.html)

This was written by Catherine Wrangham for the National Extension College (NEC). The interactive Web version, which can be accessed by anyone, is based on the printed version available from NEC. The units cover: what is language and how do we learn it? should we speak as we write? linguistic and communicative rules; pronunciation and variety in English; and words and their context.

Grammar Reference on the Web

The Internet Grammar of English
(http://www.ucl.ac.uk/english-usage/)
The Internet Grammar of English is a project based at the Survey of English Usage, University College London. It involves writing a new grammar of English and publishing it exclusively on the Web. Everyone with access to the Web will be able to use the Grammar free of charge. It is to include corpus data drawn from the British component of the International Corpus of English.

Virtual Bookshops

The Virtual Cobuild Shop
(http://titania.cobuild.collins.co.uk/cgi-bin/shop)
Gives details of relevant books on grammar, usage, confusable words, prepositions, key words in specialized subject fields, dictionaries, and others.

The Internet Bookshop
(http://www.bookshop.co/uk/)
Further information about many of the books listed in this Appendix (description and contents) may be obtained from the Internet Bookshop site.

Dictionaries for Learners and Teachers of English

The BBI Combinatory Dictionary of English: A Guide to Word Combinations. 2nd ed. John Benjamins: Amsterdam, 1997.
Cambridge International Dictionary of English, 1995.
Collins COBUILD English Language Dictionary, 1987.
A Dictionary of English Collocations. Oxford University Press: Oxford, 1994.
The Longman Dictionary of English Language and Culture, 1993.
Oxford Advanced Learner's Dictionary, 5th ed., 1996.

Books on English Language, Grammar, and Usage

Bex, T. *Variety in Written English*. Routledge: London, 1996.

Burling, R. *Patterns of Language—Structure, Variation, Change*. Academic: London, 1992.

Coates, J. *Women, Men and Language*. 2nd ed. Longman: London, 1993.

Graddol, D., and Goodman, S. *Redesigning English*. Routledge: London, 1996.

Grundy, P. *Doing Pragmatics*. Edward Arnold: London, 1995.

Halliday, M. A. K. *Introduction to Functional Grammar*. Edward Arnold: London, 1994.

Halliday, M. A. K. *Spoken and Written Language*. Oxford University Press: Oxford, 1989.

Kenworthy, J. *Language in Action: An Introduction to Modern Linguistics*. Longman: London, 1991.

Leech, G. *A–Z of English Grammar and Usage*. Edward Arnold: London, 1989.

Leech, G., and Svartvik, J. *A Communicative Grammar of English*. 2nd ed. Longman: London, 1994.

Lock, G. *Functional English Grammar—An Introduction for Second Language Teachers*. Cambridge Language Education, Cambridge University Press: Cambridge, 1995.

Tannen, D. *Gender and Conversational Interaction*. Oxford University Press: Oxford, 1993.

Todd, L., and Hancock, I. *International English Usage*. Routledge: London, 1987.

Troike, M. S. *Ethnography of Communication*. Blackwell: Oxford, 1989.

Wright, T. *Investigating English*. Edward Arnold: London, 1994.

Yule, G. *Pragmatics*. Oxford University Press: Oxford, 1996.

Books about Language Teaching and Learning

Bialystok, E. *Communication Strategies—Psychological Analysis of Second Language Use*. Blackwell: Oxford, 1990.

Carter, R., and McCarthy, M. *Vocabulary and Language Teaching*. Longman: London, 1988.

Coady, J., and Huckin, T., eds. *Second Language Vocabulary Acquisition—A Rationale for Pedagogy*. Cambridge University Press: Cambridge, 1996.

Gairns, R., and Redman, S. *Working with Words—A Guide to Teaching and Learning Vocabulary*. Cambridge Handbooks for Language Teachers. Cambridge University Press: Cambridge, 1986.

Lightbrown, P., and Spada, F. *How Languages Are Learned*. Oxford University Press: Oxford, 1993.

Littlewood, W. *Communicative Language Teaching—An Introduction. New Directions in Language Teaching.* Cambridge University Press: Cambridge, 1981.

Odlin, T. *Language Transfer—Cross-Linguistic Influence in Language Learning.* Cambridge Applied Linguistics. Cambridge University Press: Cambridge, 1990.

O'Malley, J. M., and Chamot, A. U. *Learning Strategies in Second Language Acquisition.* Cambridge Applied Linguistics. Cambridge University Press: Cambridge, 1990.

Swan, M., and Smith, B., eds. *Learner English—A Teacher's Guide to Interference and Other Problems.* Cambridge Handbooks for Language Teachers. Cambridge University Press: Cambridge, 1987.

Wierzbicka, A. *Understanding Cultures Through Their Key Words.* Oxford University Press: Oxford, 1996.

Bibliography

Aitchison, J. (1987) *Words in the Mind: An Introduction to the Mental Lexicon*. Basil Blackwell: Oxford.

Aitchison, J. (1994) "Understanding words." In G. Brown, K. Malmkjaer, A. Pollitt, and J. Williams, eds., *Language and Understanding*. Oxford University Press: Oxford.

Alpay, L., Nowlan, A., Solomon, D., Lovis, C., Baud, R., Rush, T., Scherrer, J-R. (1995) "Model-based application: the Galen structured clinical user interface." In P. Barahona, M. Stefanelli, and J. Wyatt, eds., *Artificial Intelligence in Medicine*. Springer: London.

Andersen, P. B. (1990) *A Theory of Computer Semiotics*. Cambridge University Press: Cambridge.

Anderson, B., Smyth, M., Knott, R. P., and Bergan, M. (1994) "Minimising conceptual baggage: making choices about metaphor." In G. Cockton, S. W. Draper, and G. R. S. Weir, eds., *People and Computers IX—Proceedings of HCI'94, Glasgow*. Cambridge University Press: Cambridge.

Back, M. (1996) "Cultural references in the bilingual text." *Larousse Lexicon Valley Newsletter* 1, Spring 1996.

Baker, M. (1992) *In Other Words—A Coursebook on Translation*. Routledge: London.

Barry, J. A. (1993) *Technobabble*. MIT Press: Cambridge, MA.

Batchelor, R. E., and Offord, M. H. (1993) *Using French—A Guide to Contemporary Usage*. Cambridge University Press: Cambridge.

Bell, R. T. (1991) *Translation and Translating—Theory and Practice*. Longman: London.

Bloom, C. P. (1987–88) "Procedure for obtaining and testing user-selected terminologies." *Human-Computer Interaction* 3:155–177.

Bowles, N. L., and Poon, L. W. (1985) "Effects of priming in word retrieval." *Journal of Experimental Psychology: Learning, Memory and Cognition* 11:272–283.

142   Bibliography

Bradford, A. (1988) "A planning process for online information." In S. Doheny-Farina, ed., *Effective Documentation: What We Have Learned from Research*. MIT Press: Cambridge, MA.

Brennan, R. P. (1992) *Dictionary of Scientific Literacy*. Wiley: Chichester, U.K.

Brockmann, R. J. (1986) *Writing Better Computer User Documentation: From Paper to Online*. Wiley: New York.

Brown, G., Malmkjaer, K., Pollitt, A., and Williams, J., eds. (1994) *Language and Understanding*. Oxford University Press: Oxford.

Brown, L. ed. (1993) *The New Shorter Oxford English Dictionary*. Clarendon: Oxford.

Cameron, D. (1996) *Verbal Hygiene*. Routledge: London.

Carroll, J. M. (1985) *What's In A Name? An Essay in the Psychology of Reference*. W. H. Freeman: New York.

Carroll, J. M., Mack, R. L., and Kellogg, W. A. (1990) "Interface metaphors and user interface design." In M. Helander, ed., *Handbook of Human-Computer Interaction*. North-Holland: Amsterdam.

Carroll, J. M., and Olson, J. R. (1990) "Mental models in human-computer interaction." In M. Helander, ed., *Handbook of Human-Computer Interaction*. North-Holland: Amsterdam.

Carter, R. (1987) *Vocabulary: Applied Linguistic Perspectives*. Routledge: London.

Collis, B. (1996) *Tele-Learning in a Digital World: The Future of Distance Learning*. International Thomson Computer Press: London.

Connor, U., and Johns, A. M., eds. (1990) *Coherence in Writing*. TESOL: Alexandria, VA.

Cook, G. (1989) *Discourse*. Oxford University Press: Oxford.

Cruse, D. A. (1986) *Lexical Semantics*. Cambridge University Press; Cambridge.

Crystal, D. (1987) *The Cambridge Encyclopedia of Language*. Cambridge University Press: Cambridge.

Cutts, M. (1996) *The Plain English Guide—How To Write Clearly And Communicate Better*. Oxford University Press: Oxford.

Cutts, M., and Maher, C. (1986) *The Plain English Story*. Plain English Campaign: London.

Davis, D. M. (1995) "Illusions and ambiguities in the telemedia environment: an exploration of the transformation of social roles." *Journal of Broadcasting and Electronic Media* 39:517.

Dayananda, J. Y. (1986) "Plain English in the United States." *English Today* 2:13–16.

Diaper, D. (1989) "Task Observation for HCI." In D. Diaper, ed., *Task Analysis for Human-Computer Interaction*. Ellis Horwood: Chichester, U.K.

Dix, A., Finlay, J., Abowd, G., and Beale, R. (1993) *Human-Computer Interaction*. Prentice Hall: London.

Dutta, S. (1993) *Knowledge Processing and Applied Artificial Intelligence*. Butterworth-Heinemann: Oxford.

Eberts, R. E. (1994) *User Interface Design*. Prentice Hall: Englewood Cliffs, NJ.

Eco, U. (1986) "Mirrors." In P. Bouissac, M. Herzfeld, and R. Posner, eds., *Iconicity: Essays on the Nature of Culture*. Stauffenburg Verlag: Tubingen, Germany.

Emden, J. van (1990) *A Handbook of Writing for Engineers*. Macmillan: London.

Evans, C. D., Meek, B. L., Walker, R. S., and Hopkinson, A. (1993) *User Needs in Information Technology Standards.* Butterworth-Heinemann: Oxford.

Fernandes, T. (1995) *Global Interface Design—A Guide to Designing International User Interfaces.* AP Professional: London.

Fidel, R. (1994) "User-Centered Indexing." *Journal of the American Society for Information Science* 45:572–576.

Foster, J. J. (1994) "Evaluating the effectiveness of public information symbols." *Information Design Journal* 7:183–202.

Fromkin, V., and Rodman, R. (1993) *An Introduction to Language.* 5th ed. Harcourt Brace Jovanovich: Fort Worth.

Gibbs, R. W. (1993) "Why Idioms are not Dead Metaphors." In C. Cacciari, and P. Tabossi, eds., *Idioms—Processing, Structure and Interpretation.* Lawrence Erlbaum: Hillsdale NJ.

Gookin, D., Wang, W., and Van Buren, C. (1993) *Illustrated Computer Dictionary for Dummies.* IDG Books: San Mateo, CA.

Gowers, E. (1954) *The Complete Plain Words.* H.M. Stationery Office: London.

Graddol, D., Cheshire, J, and Swann, J. (1994) *Describing Language.* 2nd ed. Open University Press: Buckingham.

Green, G. M. (1989) *Pragmatics and Natural Language Understanding.* Lawrence Erlbaum: Hillsdale, NJ.

Grimond, J., ed. (1986) *The Economist Pocket Style Book.* The Economist Publications: London.

Halliday, M. A. K. (1975) *Learning How to Mean.* Edward Arnold: London.

Halliday, M. A. K. (1978) *Language as Social Semiotic—The Social Interpretation of Language and Meaning.* Edward Arnold: London.

Harley, T. A. (1995) *The Psychology of Language—From Data to Theory.* Erlbaum (U.K.) Taylor & Francis: Hove, U.K.

Hart, A. (1989) *Knowledge Acquisition for Expert Systems.* 2nd ed. Kogan Page: London.

Hartley, J. (1985) *Designing Instructional Text.* 2nd ed. Kogan Page: London.

Hatley, R. (1996) "Buzzwords" column, The *Times Interface* supplement, 26 June 1996.

Helander, M., ed. (1990) *Handbook of Human-Computer Interaction.* North-Holland: Amsterdam.

Heller, D., and Bower, J. (1983) *Computer Confidence—A Woman's Guide.* Acropolis Books Ltd.: Washington, DC.

Hindus, D. (1991) *Conversational Paradigms in User Interfaces.* Tutorial materials from CHI'91, New Orleans, LA, April 28, 1991.

Hoey, M. (1991) *Patterns of Lexis in Text.* Oxford University Press: Oxford.

Howard, C., O'Boyle, M. W., Eastman, V., Andre, T., and Motoyama, T. (1991) "The relative effectiveness of symbols and words to convey photocopier functions." *Applied Ergonomics* 22:218–224.

Hubona, G. S., and Blanton, J. E. (1996) "Evaluating system design features." *International Journal of Human-Computer Studies* 44:93–118.

Hudson, R. (1995) *Word Meaning.* Routledge: London.

Isaacs, A., ed. (1981) *The Multilingual Computer Dictionary.* Frederick Muller Limited: London.

Jenkins, S., ed. (1992). *The Times Guide to English Style and Usage.* Times Books: London.

Jones, A., Scanlon, E., Tosunoglu, C., Rossi, S., Butcher, P., Murphy, P., and

Greenberg, J. (1996) "Evaluating CAL at the Open University: 15 years on." *Computers and Education* 26:5–15.

Kaye, A. (1992) "Learning together apart." *PLUM Report No. 30.* Institute of Educational Technology, The Open University: Milton Keynes, U.K.

Kent, P. (1994) *The Complete Idiot's Guide to the Internet.* Alpha Books/ Prentice Hall: Indianapolis, IN.

Kirkman, J. (1988) "How 'friendly' is your writing for readers around the world?" In E. Barret, ed., *Text, Context, and Hypertext.* MIT Press: Cambridge, MA.

Klein, W. (1982) "Local deixis in route directions." In R. J. Jarvella and W. Klein, eds., *Speech, Place, and Action—Studies in Deixis and Related Topics.* Wiley: Chichester, U.K.

Krol, E. (1994) *The Whole Internet—User's Guide and Catalog.* 2nd ed. O'Reilly and Associates: Sebastopol, CA.

Kukulska-Hulme, A. (1988a) "A computerized interactive vocabulary development system for advanced learners." *System* 16:163–170.

Kukulska-Hulme, A. (1988b) "Computer-assisted reference skill development." In D. Ager, ed., *Written Skills in the Modern Languages Degree,* AMLC (Aston University) in association with CILT: London.

Kukulska-Hulme, A. (1990a) "Subject knowledge in computerized dictionaries." In Thelen, M., and Lewandowska-Tomaszczyk, B., eds., "Translation and Meaning," pt. 1. *Proceedings of the Maastricht-Lodz Colloquium.* Euroterm: Maastricht.

Kukulska-Hulme, A. (1990b) "Un dictionnaire actions-acteurs pour l'informatique." *Terminogramme,* Office de la langue française, Gouvernement du Québec 55:21–24.

Kukulska-Hulme, A. (1993) Effective knowledge transfer: a terminological perspective—dismantling the jargon barrier to knowledge about computer security. Unpublished Ph.D. diss., Aston University: Birmingham, U.K.

Kukulska-Hulme, A. (1996a) "User-oriented index design for computer-based documentation." In Sharples, M., and van der Geest, T., eds., *The New Writing Environment: Writers at Work in a World of Technology.* Springer: London.

Kukulska-Hulme, A. (1996b) "Developmental testing report for the E211 course team." Open University/IET int. doc. Milton Keynes, U.K.

Kukulska-Hulme, A., and Knowles, F. (1989) "L'organisation conceptuelle des dictionnaires automatiques pour textes techniques." *META—Journal des traducteurs* vol. 34:381–397.

Kukulska-Hulme, A., and Knowles, F. (1992) "The computer as a tool for the writer: the quest for the 'Right' Word." In G. Davies, and M. Hussey, eds., *New Technology in Language Learning.* Peter Lang: Frankfurt am Main, Germany.

Kumaravadivelu, B. (1991) "Language learning tasks: teacher intention and learner interpretation." *ELT Journal* 45:98–117.

Kumaravadivelu, B. (1993) "The name of the task and the task of naming: methodological aspects of task-based pedagogy." In G. Crookes, and S. M. Gass, eds., *Tasks in a Pedagogical Context—Integrating Theory and Practice.* Multilingual Matters: Clevedon, U.K.

Lakoff, G. (1987) *Women, Fire and Dangerous Things*. University of Chicago Press, Chicago.

Langford, D. (1994) *Analysing Talk: Investigating Verbal Interaction in English*. Macmillan: London.

Langley, N. (1996) "Going native." *Computing*, 22 August 1996:20–21.

Larson, M. L. (1984) *Meaning-Based Translation: A Guide to Cross-Language Equivalence*. University Press of America: Lanham, MD.

Leech, G. (1983) *Principles of Pragmatics*. Longman: London.

Longacre, R. E. (1983) *The Grammar of Discourse*. Plenum: London.

Longley, D., and Shain, M. (1985) *Macmillan Dictionary of Information Technology*. 2nd ed. Macmillan: London.

Lytinen, S. L. (1988) "Are vague words ambiguous?" In S. L. Small, G. W. Cottrell, and M. K. Tanenhaus, eds., *Lexical Ambiguity Resolution—Perspectives from Psycholinguistics, Neuropsychology, and Artificial Intelligence*. Morgan Kaufmann: San Mateo, CA.

Mansfield, R. (1996) *Windows 95 for Busy People*. Osborne/McGraw-Hill: Berkeley, CA.

Maran, R. (1994) *Word 6 for Windows Simplified—The 3-D Visual Approach to Learning Word 6*. IDG Books: Foster City, CA.

Mason, R., ed. (1992) *Computer Conferencing: The Last Word*. Beach Holme: Victoria, B.C.

Mayhew, D. J. (1992) *Principles and Guidelines in Software User Interface Design*. Prentice Hall: Englewood Cliffs, NJ.

Meara, P. (1993) "Vocabulary acquisition." Foreword to D. Summers, ed., *Longman Language Activator Dictionary*. Longman: London.

Metcalfe, J. E. (1975) *The Right Way to Improve Your English*. Paperfronts: Kingswood, Surrey.

Mey, J. L. (1993) *Pragmatics: An Introduction*. Blackwell: Oxford.

Microsoft Corp. (1995) *The Windows Interface Guidelines for Software Design*. Microsoft Press: Redmond, WA.

Mills, G. H., and Walter, J. A. (1978) *Technical Writing*. 4th ed. Holt, Rinehart & Winston: New York.

Milroy, L. (1986) "Comprehension and context: successful communication and communicative breakdown." In G. McGregor, and R. S. White, eds., *The Art of Listening*. Croom Helm: London.

Milroy, L. (1994) "Sociolinguistics and second language learning: understanding speakers from different speech communities." In G. Brown, K. Malmkjaer, A. Pollitt, and J. Williams, eds., *Language and Understanding*. Oxford University Press: Oxford.

Monaghan, J., ed. (1987) *Grammar in the Construction of Texts*. Frances Pinter: London.

Moskel, S., Erno, J., and Shneiderman, B. (1984) "Proofreading and comprehension of text on screen and paper." Computer Science Technical Report University of Maryland: Baltimore, MD.

Newton, J. (1991) "On language, humans, and computers: an investigation into what style of language should be used in computer system messages." Submission to Bessborough essay competition, School of Cognitive and Computing Sciences, University of Sussex, U.K.

Nielsen, J. (1993) *Usability Engineering*. Academic: London.

Ogden, C. K. (1930) *Basic English: A General Introduction*. Kegan Paul, Trench & Trubner: London.

Ogden, C. K. (1968) *Basic English: International Second Language*. Rev. ed. Harcourt Brace: New York.

Ong, W. J. (1982) *Orality and Literacy—The Technologizing of the Word*. Routledge: London.

Paris, C. L. (1988) "Tailoring object descriptions to a user's level of expertise." *Computational Linguistics* 14:64–78.

Partridge, E. (1977) *A Dictionary of Catch Phrases*. Routledge & Kegan Paul: London.

Pavel, S. (1993) "Neology and phraseology as terminology-in-the-making." In H. B.Sonneveld and K. L. Loening, eds., *Terminology: Applications in Interdisciplinary Communication*. John Benjamins: Amsterdam.

Pavel, S. (1994) *Guide to Phraseology Research in Languages for Special Purposes, Terminology and Documentation Directorate*. Translation Bureau: Montreal.

Pelc, J. (1986) "Iconicity—iconic signs or iconic uses of signs?" In P. Bouissac, M. Herzfeld, and R. Posner, eds., *Iconicity: Essays on the Nature of Culture*. Stauffenburg Verlag: Tubingen, Germany.

Phillips, M. D., Bashinski, H. S., Ammerman, H. L., and Fligg, C. M. (1990) "A task analytic approach to dialogue design." In M. Helander, ed., *Handbook of Human-Computer Interaction*. North-Holland: Amsterdam.

Poole, L. (1994) *Macworld System 7.5 Bible*. 3rd ed. IDG Books: Foster City, CA.

Reese, R. A. (1996) "Word processing," submitted to *Baskerville*, newsletter of the U.K. TeX User Group and part of unpublished Ph.D. research at the University of Hull, U.K.

Richards, I. A. (1943) *Basic English and Its Uses*. Kegan Paul, Trench and Tubner: London.

Rogers, Y., and Osborne, D. (1987) "Pictorial communication of abstract verbs in relation to human-computer interaction." *British Journal of Psychology* 78:99–112.

Room, A. (1985) *Dictionary of Confusing Words and Meanings*. Routledge & Kegan Paul: London.

Rosch, E. (1975) "Cognitive representation of semantic categories." *Journal of Experimental Psychology: General* no. 104:192–233.

Rosenberg, D., and Hutchison, C., eds. (1994) *Design Issues in CSCW*. Springer-Verlag: London.

Rosenberg, J. M. (1987) *Dictionary of Computers, Information Processing and Telecommunications*. 2nd ed. Wiley: Chichester, U.K.

Rowntree, D. (1981) *Developing Courses for Students*. Paul Chapman: London.

Sager, J. (1990) *A Practical Course in Terminology Processing*. John Benjamins: Amsterdam.

Sager, J. (1994) *Language Engineering and Translation: Consequences of Automation*. John Benjamins: Amsterdam.

Saugstad, P. (1977) *A Theory of Communication and Use of Language*. Universitetsforlaget: Oslo.

Scollon, R., and Scollon, S. W. (1995) *Intercultural Communication—A Discourse Approach*. Blackwell: Oxford.

Searle, J. (1970) *Speech Acts*. Cambridge University Press: Cambridge.

Shorter Oxford English Dictionary (1983). Guild Publishing: Oxford.

Sides, C. (1984) *How to Write Papers and Reports about Computer Technology*. ISI: Philadelphia, PA.

Sinclair, J. (1984) "Naturalness in language." In J. Aarts and W. Meijs, eds., *Corpus Linguistics*: Rodopi. Amsterdam.

Sinclair, J. (1991) *Corpus, Concordance, Collocation*. Oxford University Press: Oxford.

Singer, R. (1995) "Usability study of the scholar's desktop." *Biodiversity Evaluation Studies Internal Report No.1*. The Open University: Milton Keynes, U.K.

Smith, L. E. (1987) *Discourse Across Cultures—Strategies in World Englishes*. Prentice Hall: London.

Smith, R. (1992) *Powerpoint 3.0 Training Bideo, Tape 1*. MacAcademy, Florida Marketing Intern., Inc.

Smith, S. L. (1990) "Standards versus guidelines for designing user interface software." In M. Helander, ed., *Handbook of Human-Computer Interaction*. North-Holland: Amsterdam.

Sorensen, E. K. (1992) "Metaphors and the design of the human interface." In A. R. Kaye, ed., *Collaborative Learning Through Computer Conferencing—The Najaden Papers*. Springer-Verlag: London.

Spears, R. A. (1991) *NTC's Dictionary of Grammar Terminology*. National Textbook Company: Lincolnwood (Chicago), IL.

Stokes, A. V. (1985) *Concise Encyclopaedia of Information Technology*. 2nd ed. Gower: Aldershot.

Summers, D., ed. (1993) *Longman Language Activator Dictionary*. Longman: London.

Swann, J. (1992) *Girls, Boys and Language*. Blackwell: Oxford.

Tanz, C. (1980) *Studies in the Acquisition of Deictic Terms*. Cambridge University Press, Cambridge, U.K.

Tevis, J. (1989) *Desktop Publishing with WordPerfect 5.0*. Wiley: Chichester, U.K.

Tonfoni, G. (1994) *Writing as a Visual Art*. Intellect Books: Oxford.

Trudgill, P., and Hannah, J. (1994) *International English—A Guide to the Varieties of Standard English*. 3rd ed. Edward Arnold: London.

Truss, L. (1996) "Save me from manual labour." *The Times Interface Supplement*, 21/2/96.

Urdang, L., and La Roche, N., eds. (1980) *Picturesque Expressions—A Thematic Dictionary*. Gale Research Company: Detroit, MI.

Vincent, T. (1997) *Design Guidelines & WWW Design Guidelines for Maximising Accessibility*. Open University Multimedia Enabling Technologies (MET) documents, http://met.open.ac.uk/

Waern, Y. (1989) *Cognitive Aspects of Computer Supported Tasks*. Wiley: Chichester, U.K.

Wales, K. (1989) *A Dictionary of Stylistics*. Longman: London.

Watson, M. (1996) "The gender issue: what you see is what you get—or is it?" *Centre for Language and Communications occasional paper No. 49*, Open University School of Education: Milton Keynes, U.K.

Wessel, A. E. (1975) *Computer-Aided Information Retrieval*. Melville: Los Angeles, CA.

Wiklund, M. E., ed. (1994) *Usability in Practice—How Companies Develop User-Friendly Products*. Academic: London.

Williams, R., and Cummings, S. (1993) *Jargon: An Informal Dictionary of Computer Terms*. Peachpit Press: Berkeley, CA.

Willis, D. (1991) *Collins Cobuild Student's Grammar*. Collins ELT/HarperCollins: London.

Wilson, C. E., Loring, B. A., Conte, L., and Stanley, K. (1994) "Usability engineering at Dun & Bradstreet software." In Wiklund, ed., *Usability in Practice—How Companies Develop User-Friendly Products*. Academic: London.

Winnett, M., Malyan, R., and Barnwell, P. (1994) "ShareLib: a toolkit for CSCW applications programming using X Windows." In Rosenberg and Hutchison, eds., *Design Issues in CSCW*. Springer Verlag: London.

Subject Index

User Interface Index

This additional index, intended for designers and developers, lists some words found in interfaces to operating systems and applications. Use this index to check particular words that you are planning to incorporate in new user interfaces or documentation.

Printed in the United Kingdom
by Lightning Source UK Ltd.
100798UKS00001B/69